THE *REAL BOOK* ABOUT

INVENTIONS

THE *REAL BOOK* ABOUT

INVENTIONS

BY

SAMUEL EPSTEIN

AND

BERYL WILLIAMS

ILLUSTRATED BY LÁSZLO ROTH

EDITED BY HELEN HOKE

GARDEN CITY BOOKS

GARDEN CITY, NEW YORK

BY ARRANGEMENT WITH FRANKLIN WATTS, INC.

1951

GARDEN CITY BOOKS

PRINTED IN THE UNITED STATES OF AMERICA
BY THE COUNTRY LIFE PRESS

CONTENTS

THE *REAL BOOK* ABOUT
INVENTIONS

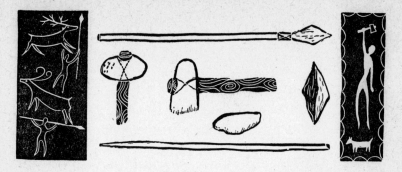

1. THE TOOLS CAME FIRST

It's always fun to pretend—to imagine ourselves great heroes. In our minds we can win battles, find buried treasure, be great musicians or actors, discover new continents—do any of a hundred difficult things. We simply decide what kind of hero we want to be, and then we go on spinning daydreams by the hour.

But there's one kind of hero we find it difficult to copy, even in our imagination, because we can't quite imagine what he did. There was so little he *could* do. He was Prehistoric Man.

Still, we might try it the next time the alarm clock wakes us early some morning. We might pretend we are Prehistoric Man waking up 500,000 years ago.

500,000 Years Ago

Of course there are no written records of life in that ancient time. That's why we call it prehistoric—meaning *before history*. But we have a rough idea of the kind of life he woke up to. It wasn't an easy one.

In the first place there was no alarm clock to wake him.

11

How could there be? Metals were unknown and no one had even thought to invent a wheel. And what kind of an alarm clock can you build without wheels and steel springs?

So we'll have to imagine that he's been awakened by the roaring of some ferocious beast outside the house. But wait—there weren't any houses yet. He's living in a cave.

Very well then: he hears a roaring outside the cave and, being a brave hero, throws back his warm blanket and . . .

But no! There is no blanket. No one yet knows about wool or how to weave it into cloth. And no one yet knows about cotton or silk or linen and so there are no clothes either.

Not having to dress saves him a lot of time. He reaches for his gun . . . Impossible! No one has yet invented guns. It is with only his bare hands for weapons that he leaps to his feet and heads for the mouth of the cave. He stumbles over rocks in the dark because nobody has devised any form of light other than the campfire and his campfire has gone out.

He mutters to himself when he sees that the fire is dead. He knows that now he will have to do without any fire until lightning strikes another tree and sets it aflame. Unfortunately for him nobody has yet thought of how to start a fire by rubbing two sticks together, or by any other method.

Finally he reaches the mouth of the cave. And there in the darkness, only a short distance away, he sees two evil, gleaming eyes. He hears the savage growl in the beast's throat. He faces the enemy, hands clenched, muscles tensed for the leap.

12

But just before he hurls himself forward, a sharp pain reminds him that he hurt his hand the day before trying to smash a nut. He realizes that with only one good hand he is no match for this beast.

A Stone to Strike With

Suddenly he has an idea. If he could use something instead of that bruised and aching hand . . .

He gropes on the ground. His fingers close over a rock that fits neatly into his palm. It is much harder than a fist. He leaps forward, the rock held high. It comes down hard. It strikes squarely. He has vanquished the enemy. And he has become a hero—perhaps the greatest hero the world has ever known.

Not for killing the beast—many beasts have been killed before. He is a hero because he is the first person to have used something other than his own body to do his work.

That stone in his hand is much more than a stone. It is the forerunner of the hammer, and of all the tools man's ingenuity has devised since that dim day so long ago. He has started civilization on its way.

Discoveries Come First

The Prehistoric Man who first used a rock as a weapon didn't really invent anything; he made a discovery. He discovered that a stone held in the hand did more than protect his hand from injury; it also increased the power of his blow. A stone is harder and heavier than a hand. Therefore it could strike harder and more heavily.

Prehistoric Man was strong—stronger than the man of today. He had to be strong in order to survive in his wild and dangerous world.

But his enemies were even stronger—the saber-toothed tiger, the huge woolly rhinoceros, the great elephant-like creature called a mammoth. Any one of them could kill a man with a single blow or tear him apart with fierce claws or tusks. Yet man had to compete with these enemies for food and had to protect himself from their attack.

Two important things made man seem stronger than he was. First, he stood upright, while his enemies walked on four feet. Thus man could use his hands—his "forefeet"—to protect himself and to perform many tasks.

Second, he had a better brain than his enemies had. He could think better than they could. It was his brain that discovered how a stone could be used instead of a fist.

A Sharp Edge and a Sharp Point

His brain led him to two more very important discoveries.

He discovered that a sharp-edged stone could serve him as well as sharp claws served his enemies. With a sharp stone he could cut up the animals he killed for food. With a sharp stone he could even scrape the hide clean and use an animal skin as a protection from the cold. His simple sharp-edged stone was the beginnings of the tool we call a knife.

He also discovered that he could use a stick in the same way his enemies used their tusks—to dig up roots that were good to eat. He learned that the best stick for digging was one that had a pointed end like a mammoth's tusk. Often he looked for a long time to find a stick that had a sharp point. And finally he learned how to point the tip of a stick with his sharp stone.

The pointed stick was a great help

Now he had three important discoveries: a stone to strike with, a sharp-edged stone, and a pointed stick. He would, eventually, do a great many things with these simple objects.

The First Invention

And one day man made a real invention.

He had been using his heavy stone for a long time—for hundreds, perhaps thousands of years. But he was still in great danger. He had to come very close to an enemy in order to strike him with a stone. He had to come so close that often the enemy struck him before his stone could do its work.

Suppose—man's brain suggested one day—suppose he

fastened the rock to a stick. Then he could stand some distance away from an enemy and still strike at him.

With strips torn from one of his animal hides he clumsily tied a stone to a stout branch. When it was well fastened he tried swinging the stick over his head and letting the stone strike against a tree. It made a good solid thump. It was safer to use than a stone. And it struck much harder than a stone held in the hand because a stone at the end of a stick moved faster.

He struck the tree again and felt very proud of himself. And he should have been proud. He had taken two natural objects—a stone and a stick—and had combined them to form something which never existed before. He had made the first hammer.

Man had become a true inventor!

How Inventions Come About

But it is important to remember how this invention came about. First, the stones and sticks had to exist, so they could be discovered and made use of. Second, there had to be a need; man's brain went to work because man needed help in his fight for survival. And, third, the inventor had to know what others before him had done—how they had used stones in order to strike heavy blows.

Man's brain—man's ingenuity—invented the hammer. But the invention could not have happened without those other three things: the raw material, the need, and the work of earlier men. All inventions, even today, depend on those same three things. They are very important to remember.

When we say that necessity is the mother of invention, we must not forget the other two things. Perhaps we could say that the two others—the raw material and the work of earlier men—are, together, the father of invention.

How the Axe Came About

We can see, for example, how all three were necessary to bring about the invention of the axe.

Sharp stones existed and man discovered their usefulness.

Then there came a time when man needed to do something which his sharpest stone could not do. Perhaps he needed to cut down a tree, and he found that no matter how hard he struck it with his stone, he could make only scratches in the tree's bark.

But suddenly he remembered that tying a stick to a stone increased the strength of the stone's blow. And so he tied a stick to his sharp stone and was able to chop the tree down with little difficulty.

He had made another important invention.

The materials, the need, the work that has gone before —they all appear in the story of every invention.

Where the Materials Came From

The materials have always existed.

The metals, the chemicals—all the vast number of things which go into our most complex inventions today —have always been a part of the earth.

Some of them were hidden so well that it took man many years to find them. Today we dig thousands of feet into the earth to find minerals or oil, and go deep into the ocean to bring up certain plants or fish which provide us with things we need.

Other materials—like iron, for example—were so mixed up with other things that it took man many years to separate them out so they could be useful in themselves.

Today we sift through tons of rock in order to obtain a tiny pinch of radium or platinum. Today we know that although a certain plant may be poisonous if eaten whole, some one part of it—separated out by skilled scientists—may provide us with a vitamin to keep us well, or a medicine to cure us of disease.

Still other things—like fire and electricity—were so terrifying in their natural state that it took man many years to learn to tame and control them for his own use. To early man lightning was a danger; today we know lightning is a form of electricity—and electricity is one of our most valuable possessions. Fire, that can destroy vast forests, is usually our faithful servant. We can summon it today simply by striking a match.

All things, in one form or another, were here from the very beginning. Slowly man learned to make use of them, as his needs increased.

What Did Early Man Need?

What kind of things did man need in those days?

Five hundred thousand years ago—even as recently as thirty thousand years ago—man was what we call a forager; he searched for his food. He searched for animals and killed them for meat. He searched for fish, and caught them with his bare hands. He searched for berries and fruits and certain vegetables. And, a little later, he discovered that grains—like wheat and barley—were also good for food.

Of course it wasn't always easy to catch and kill animals for food. Man especially liked the meat of the bison and the small horse that roamed the world then—but the bison and the horse could both run very fast, and it was difficult to catch them. Man could seldom get close enough to strike at either a horse or a bison with a stone or hammer.

He tried to throw stones at them, and sometimes he was lucky—but not very often. A light stone, which he could throw a long distance, was not heavy enough to kill. And a heavy stone couldn't be thrown very far.

The Spear

Perhaps, one day, a man sat at the edge of a clearing looking at the herd of bison feeding some distance away. The man was hungry. If he could kill one of those bison he would have enough for a great feast. But if he ventured into the clearing they would see him and run off.

Perhaps he sat for a long time, growing more and more hungry. He *needed* food. He began to think of all the ways man had already invented to kill animals. And suddenly he thought of a new way, based on those old ones.

He looked around until he found a stone with a sharp point. Next he pulled a branch from a tree—a long straight

19

branch—and trimmed off the twigs. Then, with some long tough vines, he fastened the pointed stone to the very end of the branch.

The spear

Holding his new weapon in his hand he advanced to the edge of the clearing. He raised the long stone-tipped shaft aloft and hurled it at the nearest animal. To his great delight it flew straight to its target, point first. The stone buried itself in the bison's flesh, and the animal fell.

Man had a new source of food. He had a new weapon. He had invented the spear.

Man Learns to Plant

His need led him to invent other uses for that sharp point.

Sometimes, when he walked long weary miles to the place where he had once before found berries or grains, he discovered that wandering animals had already eaten them all. Man wished there were more of those berries and grains, and that they were nearer the stream where he lived in his cave. There would be more next year, of course: he learned that berries and grains came up each spring from the seeds that dropped in the fall.

And suddenly the idea came to him: why couldn't he carry the seeds home and put them in the ground close to his cave? Why couldn't he make a small hole in the ground with a sharpened stick and drop the seeds in? This is just what he did.

The first seeds he planted with his sharp stick were the beginning of today's great farms.

Man Learns to Sew

Early man discovered that a sharp point could make holes in many other things.

Man learns to sew

When he wandered into the mountains, where it was cold, he needed more protection than a single animal skin could give him. So he punched holes in two animal skins with a sharp stone, or a sharp sliver of bone, and tied them together with thongs run through the holes.

Later he realized that he could make a hole in that thin sliver of bone by working away at it with a sharply pointed stone. He pulled a long thong through the hole and then—when he pushed the bone through his skins to make holes in them—the thong traveled along with the bone and held the skins tightly together. Man had learned to sew; he had invented the needle.

The First Inventions Were Important

Today those first simple tools—the hammer, the sharp edge, the sharp point—seem too simple to be worth remembering. But without them man would probably have perished long ago, destroyed by his enemies.

With them he created the world we know.

The Hammer Today

Today there is a hammer in every carpenter's hand. A huge hammer, driven by power, smashes rocks in quarries. Our riveting machine is a kind of hammer. The great punch press that molds the metal bodies of our automobiles is another kind of hammer. The geologist's little hammer, tapping away at rocks, has helped man discover many of the metals he uses today—the metals that make his hammers, among many other things.

The Sharp Edge Today

Man's first sharp-edged rock is also the ancestor of many of the tools that make life possible today. The saw that cuts lumber for our houses, our knives and scissors,

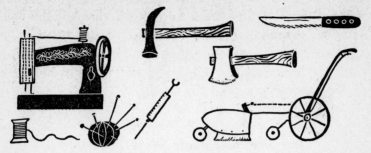

Sharp points and sharp edges today

all came from that sharp stone. And so did the butcher's cleaver and the farmer's reaper.

The Sharp Point Today

And the sharp point has developed into our plow and our drill as well as our needle.

Today's power-driven plows prepare the vast acres that feed the people of the earth.

Today's mines are great holes in the earth made by power-driven points we call drills. They provide the materials for our machines, our automobiles, our airplanes, our pots and pans—for thousands of articles we see and use each hour. And drills make wells—the holes in the earth from which we get water and oil.

Today's sewing machines drive slender steel needles swiftly up and down, stitching the seams of millions of garments. A delicate little glass needle we call a hypodermic needle helps us conquer pain and disease.

We owe a great deal to early man. His inventions were simple, but they were very important.

Early man was a hero. He was a great inventor.

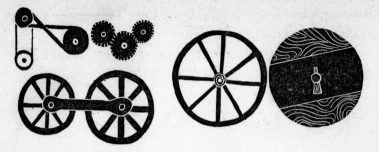

2. THE WHEEL

What is man's single most important invention? The steam engine? The airplane? Television?

All these—and many more—are very important, of course. But there is one single invention that made these and almost all other inventions possible.

It is the wheel.

Perhaps you've never stopped to think how important the wheel is. But look around you. With a moment's thought you will realize that wheels were necessary for the making of almost every object you see—at home, at school, in the street.

The lumber for our houses was cut by a circular saw—which is a kind of wheel. The power for those saws came from machines that can't operate without wheels. And the lumber was probably brought to us by trains or trucks. Even ships and airplanes have wheels, in their engines.

The cement for our pavements was ground by grinding wheels. We have enough food because we have farm machinery that uses wheels. And there are wheels in the factories that make that machinery—as there are wheels in almost all factories.

Some of the wheels we use today—in a big power plant,

for example—weigh hundreds of tons. Others—in a wrist watch—are almost too small to see.

But big or little, wherever they are, they all turn. That is the important thing about a wheel: it turns.

Before There Was a Wheel

Of course man didn't always have wheels. For thousands of years—even after there were hammers and edged tools—no one had figured out this most important invention.

Early man foraged for his food

Why not?

For a long time there was no need for wheels.

Primitive man, as he foraged food, never traveled very far at one time, and had little to carry. His possessions were his spear, his club, his knife, and the animal skin on his back. He could manage very well without anything to ride in, or anything to help him carry what he owned.

But then, as the centuries rolled by, man discovered that berries and grains could be planted and made to grow. And this meant that he could build a shelter in

25

some pleasant place and stay there, growing part of his food instead of roaming around to look for it.

Of course he still hunted animals for meat. But now women were left at home, to tend the fields, and the hunters returned at night to their little skin or bark houses, or their caves.

This new kind of living was pleasanter in many ways. People had time to learn about new things.

They made better tools.

They made clay pots for cooking.

But always there came a time when they had to leave one home and move to a new one. Sometimes it was because there were no animals left in the neighborhood. Sometimes it was because they had planted crops in the same ground for several years, and the soil had worn out. And they discovered that moving was not quite so simple as it had been in their early foraging days.

They had their supplies of grain to carry, their new tools, and their new pots. All these things together made a heavy load on a man's back.

The Pack Animal

Finally man began to tame some of the wild animals that roamed in the forests and over the plains. And after he had done that he shifted his loads to an animal's back.

In India the elephant got the job. In Arabia the camel took up man's burden. In South America it was the llama. Europe, parts of Asia, and northern Africa had the horse.

Years and centuries passed. Man learned more about the soil. He no longer had to move to a new place every few years. He became more settled and more civilized. He began to live in groups—in villages.

But even though man was not moving his home and family so frequently, he found it more and more necessary to move—to carry—other things.

Man put the elephant to work

Firewood was one. The people in a village soon burned up all the nearby supply, and after that they had to haul their wood from distant forests.

Then, too, in time, the people in one village found that they could trade with people in other villages. Firewood could be exchanged for grain; salt and fish could be exchanged for pottery or animal hides.

Traders wore paths over the hills and through the forests, as they and their animals went back and forth with their goods year after year. Those paths were the world's first roads.

But still man had no wheel.

Man Invents the Drag

After a while, however, it did occur to him that it is sometimes easier to *slide* a thing from one place to an-

27

other than to pick it up and carry it. And so he invented a simple device called a *drag*.

You may have seen pictures of a drag. Certain American Indians still used them, not so long ago, to carry their wigwams and other possessions. And even today, in some parts of Asia, drags are still in use.

Man invented the drag

The drag was made by fastening the ends of two slender poles to a strap slung across a horse's shoulders. The poles—one on each side of the horse—dragged along the ground behind him, and a pack could be laid across them and lashed into place.

A drag could transport a much bulkier load than a horse could carry on his back.

The Drag Becomes a Sled

In some parts of the ancient world the drag took on a different form; it became what we call a *sled*. Sleds of ten or maybe twenty thousand years ago looked rather like the horse-drawn sleds we still sometimes see today, except that the old ones were more crudely made.

Sleds became popular in the north country, where there was lots of snow and ice, and also in the sandy plains of certain parts of Asia. Dogs probably pulled the sleds across the northern snows, as they do to this day. Heavy oxen dragged sleds across the Asiatic plains.

The Beginning of the Wheel

Just when or how the first wheel appeared is a mystery.

Man may have noticed that a log too heavy to lift, and even too heavy to drag, could easily be rolled. Or, perhaps, while moving heavy stones, he noticed how much more easily a round stone could be rolled than a flat stone dragged or lifted.

In any case sometime, somewhere, he realized this one important fact: round objects could be moved more easily than any other kind. And he decided he could use round objects to help him move other things.

The First Wheel Was a Roller

Probably the first form of the wheel was simply a log used as a roller. But soon man developed a crude sort of wagon, using a log roller instead of wheels.

We don't know exactly what this first wagon looked like. But the scientists who study the lives of ancient peoples have figured out that it was probably a square wooden frame with holes in the sides. The log which was used as a wheel was carved away at the ends, so that it had the shape of a rolling pin. The thin ends of the log then fitted into the holes.

The trimmed-down ends of the log formed what we now call an *axle*. The holes in the frame formed what we now call a *bearing*.

This simple wagon, or cart, was a great improvement over the drag and the sled. With it an animal, or a man, could pull much heavier loads than before.

But as time went by man began to realize that his cart wasn't as good as it might be. The log roller made it very

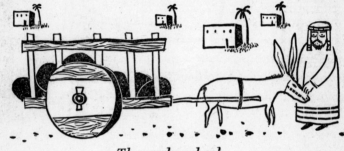

The early wheel

heavy. In fact the cart was often many times heavier than the burden it could carry.

The First Wheel

Man wondered how to improve his cart—and one day he had a very clever idea. He went out into the woods, cut down a big tree and hacked two pieces from its trunk —two round slices or disks of wood.

In the center of each disk he made a round hole.

Next he removed the frame of his cart from its roller. He fastened to the bottom of the frame a thin log, with its ends sticking beyond the frame on either side. Over

those ends he fitted his great slices of wood, like dough-
nuts on a stick.

His round slices of wood were wheels—the first real
wheels ever made.

His new cart was light. It could roll over many obstacles that would have stopped a heavy roller. It could
be turned easily around corners.

Roman chariot

But man still wasn't satisfied. Even the disk wheels
were very heavy. He decided to make them lighter.

The First Spoked Wheel

He cut some holes in his wooden wheel, between its
center and its edge. It was lighter—which was what he
wanted—and it was still strong. And so he cut out a few
more holes—and then a few more again. Finally his once-
solid wheel looked very much like a piece of swiss cheese.

And suddenly man said to himself, "Why should I
make a solid wheel—and then cut all these holes in it until
there is nothing left but narrow strips? Why can't I start
with narrow pieces, and fit them together?"

31

And he did.

His wheel had a solid piece in the center, through which the axle would fit. We call that center piece a *hub*.

Stuck into this hub, all around it, were strong sticks. We call them *spokes*.

Wheels carry civilization forward

And fastened to the outer ends of the spokes was a rim of wood, made of small curved pieces fastened together to make a complete circle. We call this circle a *rim*.

Now man had a true, spoked wheel.

The Importance of the Wheel

It is this wheel which made our civilization possible. It gave the Romans their chariots. It gave our own pioneers their covered wagons. It gives us our automobiles, trucks, busses, and railroads today. We travel on wheels.

But the wheel has been useful for many other things too. It gives us power.

The water-wheel, the electric generator, the steam turbine—all are special kinds of wheels.

Wheels transfer power too—when they are put to work in the form of pulleys and gears. Without wheels there would be no machines—no factories.

Man's progress has rolled swiftly forward, carried on by the turning of his greatest invention—the wheel.

3. POWER: DOING THE WORLD'S WORK

When primitive man wanted something done, *he* had to do it.

When he wanted flour, he pounded grain between rocks. When his field needed plowing, he dragged a forked stick through the earth. If he wanted to cross a river or a lake, he paddled his heavy dugout over the water.

For thousands of years primitive man lived by his own strength. He could survive only if he was very strong.

Gradually man discovered that there is strength in other things besides his own muscles. He learned by watching a stiff breeze bend the grass and send the leaves spiraling around or by seeing a stormy gale uproot huge trees that there is great strength in the wind. He saw how rushing streams and pounding waves could carry along logs and animals and even man himself, and he found that there is great strength in water.

This strength is called *power*. Because he has learned how to use power, today man can erect towering skyscrapers, span raging rivers with mile-long bridges, speed over the earth and on the sea and through the air in trains and automobiles, ships and airplanes.

34

Power is invisible.

We can see the work that power does for us, but we can't see the power itself. We press a button and an electric bulb lights up—but we can't see the electricity in the wires. We get into a car and drive off—but we don't see the power in the gasoline.

Sometimes, because we can't see power, we are likely to take for granted that it is always there, ready to serve us. But when it *isn't* there—when we press a button and the lamp doesn't light, or when a car breaks down miles

Animals turned millstones

from the nearest town—then we suddenly realize that without power we would be no better off than the man who lived thousands of years ago.

Animal Power

Primitive man was his own source of power. He depended on the strength of his own muscles to survive.

Then his ingenuity led him to a way to increase his strength.

The first animals that man captured alive were kept as

35

a food supply for the days when hunting was bad. But the baby camels, horses and buffalo born in captivity were not so wild as their parents. They became what we call *domesticated* animals.

And man realized that he could use some of these animals to help him with his heavy work. He harnessed them to pull his plows, to lift water from his wells. Animals turned great millstones to grind his flour—they even threshed his grain. They carried man's burdens and man himself; they pulled his drags, his sleds, and finally his carts and wagons.

Man now had two sources of power: his own muscles and those of his animals. We call both these powers *animate,* from the Latin word *anima,* meaning the *breath of life*. All animate power comes from living muscles.

Man still had no inanimate power—power that does not come from living muscles.

Wind Power

Man's first inanimate power was the wind.

Of course, he had known for many hundreds of years that there was great strength in the wind. He had seen its power during storms, but as he cowered in his shelter and watched a hurricane uproot tremendous trees he thought that the wind was an evil demon bent on destroying the world. It took a long time for man to realize that he could make the wind work for him.

As far as we know, his first use of it was to help him move his boats through the water. The name of the man who made the first sails will never be known, but he was a great inventor. Almost seven thousand years ago men were using small sails on their boats.

The use of the wind on land, to turn wheels, came hundreds of years later.

Man's first wind-wheels were called *windmills,* because they were used to turn millstones to grind grain. The

Windmills ground man's flour

wheels were crude clumsy affairs, with cloth-covered arms that looked very much like the sails on his boats. They were set up on top of stone or wooden towers, and they revolved slowly even in a good wind.

Even those slow early windmills were very useful, however. All over Europe—in what is now Germany, Belgium, France, the Netherlands and England—they began to appear. Later, when colonists came to America, windmills were built here too. A few of them still stand.

But the modern windmill, widely used today, is very different from those early ones. Slender steel blades have replaced the big cloth sails. Light steel towers are used instead of heavy wood or stone ones. Most of today's windmills are used for pumping water, but some of them turn electric generators to supply farms with electricity.

Man took a great step forward when he learned to use the wind. But the wind doesn't always blow—and without wind both sails and windmills are useless.

Fortunately man discovered another, steadier source of power.

Water Power

The power of falling or rushing water, like the power of the wind, was always in the world. All man had to do was to find a way to use it. But it took him much longer to put water to work than it did for him to harness the wind to move his boats.

Water goes to work

It wasn't until the time of Julius Caesar—about two thousand years ago—that man first used the force of a rapidly flowing stream to work for him. Paddles were attached to the rim of a wheel and the force of the water falling on these caused the wheel to turn. The shaft, or axle, of the paddle wheel, attached to a millstone for grinding flour, could do the work of many men.

The water wheel wasn't widely used at first, because

there were thousands of slaves in Rome at that time and their masters didn't care much about saving labor. But as the number of slaves decreased, water wheels became more important. By the year 300 they were quite common in Rome. And from Rome they spread throughout the populated lands of the world. Water wheels were built wherever there were streams to operate them.

But water, like the wind, is not always present. Streams that are rushing torrents in the spring may be tiny trickles in the dry summer months. Unlike wind, however, water can be stored. So man began to build dams—to create ponds and lakes, so that he would have water to turn his wheels during the dry season.

Man also learned how to improve his wheels. They grew larger and more powerful—many times more powerful than the best windmill.

Water wheels were mainly of two kinds.

One was called an *overshot* wheel: the water flowed over the top of the wheel and turned it by weight. This kind of wheel is seldom used today.

The other was called an *undershot* wheel: the water struck the wheel's paddles from underneath, and drove them up and around.

The huge, highly efficient water turbine, in use today at the world's great dams, is the most modern form of that little paddle wheel the Romans used two thousand years ago. The enormous power of the turbine is used to generate electricity which can be carried over wires for use hundreds of miles away.

The power of the early water wheel, of course, had to be used right where it was made. This wasn't always convenient; man sometimes needed power at places where there were no rivers or streams. By the year 1600 this need had become very great.

So man began to seek a new kind of power—a power that he could create for himself wherever he needed it.

For a while he didn't realize that it too already existed —right in his own kitchen.

Hero's Steam Engine

The power of steam had been ready for man as soon as he began to use fire. But for thousands of years he watched steam lifting the lid of his cooking pot—and never thought of using this invisible power to help him do his work.

Even when the inventive genius Hero made a real steam engine, in the year 120 B.C., other men treated it as only a curious toy. They watched it spin, but never

Hero's steam engine

thought of putting it to use. So far as we know even the inventor himself regarded his engine as nothing more than a plaything.

Hero's steam engine was simple.

It was a hollow metal ball, with two thin arms—like two

spouts on a teakettle. The ball was hung between two pivots, so that it could revolve. When steam from a boiling pot was forced into the ball, through the hollow pivots, it came out through the tiny spouts. The force of the two jets of steam, on opposite sides of the ball, made it spin merrily around.

The rockets we set off on the Fourth of July, and the sprinklers that spin around on our lawns, also work by this principle. So do jet-propelled planes.

But Hero's engine, like most toys, amused men for a while and was shortly forgotten.

Branca's Steam Engine

More than 1700 years later an Italian named Branca finally had an astounding idea: *steam power could do work*.

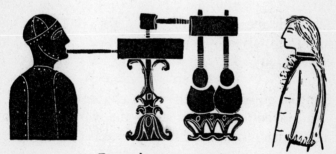

Branca's steam engine

He promptly designed a curious little engine which he planned to use to pound drugs to powder. Powdering drugs may not seem to us very important work, but at least it was *work*.

Steam for the engine was made in a boiler shaped like

a man's head and chest. The steam emerged from the man's mouth, struck a small paddle wheel and spun it around. The axle of the wheel operated two weights which rose and fell—and each time they fell they struck the drugs in a pair of bowls.

Hero's steam engine, and Branca's, were the clues man found when he finally started his serious search for a new kind of power.

Water in the Mines

In England about 1650 the search was very intense. One job especially needed a new kind of power. English coal mines were filling up with water; and, unless the water could be pumped out, the coal couldn't be dug and England would have no fuel.

For a long time the mines had been kept dry by the use of horses and oxen to lift the water out in huge buckets attached to ropes. But as the shafts were dug deeper, the water ran in faster. In some mines hundreds of animals worked twenty-four hours a day to keep ahead of the flood.

The coal miners knew they were fighting a losing battle. And inventors—remembering the work of Hero and Branca—began to wonder if they couldn't harness steam instead of horses.

In 1663 a British nobleman named Edward Somerset succeeded in putting steam to work; he invented a crude steam engine which could force water upward, through a pipe, for a distance of forty feet.

The mines were deeper than that, of course. Somerset didn't solve their problem. But his engine proved that steam could do the *kind* of work the miners wanted done.

Experimenting with steam was dangerous in those days. Boilers blew up, pipes burst. Injuries were frequent and serious. But men went on building boilers and studying the power of steam. Somerset's work had encouraged them.

The Safety Valve

Denis Papin, in France, was one of those men. One of the first and most important things he did was to make steam boilers safer; he invented what we call a *safety valve*.

This device—used in every steam boiler to this day—permits steam to escape whenever there is more of it than a boiler can safely hold. Fewer boilers burst after Papin's invention was widely used.

Papin's Piston

But Papin made another and even more important invention. About 1690, ten years after he made the first safety valve, he invented a steam engine which used a *piston* and a *cylinder*.

We can best understand how this engine worked if we think of a pea shooter: the pea is the piston, and the shooter is the cylinder. When we blow in one end of a pea shooter, our breath forces the pea out at the other end.

Papin's cylinder was a metal tube; his piston was a metal disk that fitted snugly inside it. When Papin blew steam into the bottom of his cylinder, the piston was forced upward. When the steam cooled, and changed back into water, the piston came down.

It didn't take long for somebody to realize that this up-and-down motion of the piston could be useful in emptying the water out of the mines.

A Steam Engine Empties the Mines

In 1705 Thomas Newcomen, an English blacksmith, fastened a steam-driven piston to one end of a huge see-saw. The other end of the see-saw was connected, by a long rod, to a pump deep in a coal mine. Each time the piston moved up, the rod moved down. Each time the piston came down, the rod moved up—bringing with it great quantities of water.

Newcomen's engine saved the coal mines. England was grateful.

It is true that it was slow in operation. It took a long time for the steam to cool off—to bring the piston down and the pump-rod up. The engine could make only 12 or 15 strokes a minute.

But nearly seventy-five years went by before anyone figured out a better kind of steam engine for the mines.

James Watt and His Engine

It was James Watt who finally did. His piston-driven steam engine was so good that we still use it today, with very little change.

James Watt was an instrument maker—a fine machinist

who could make or repair the most delicate mechanism. He might have refused scornfully when he was asked, one day, to repair a clumsy Newcomen engine. But all mechanical things interested him, and he agreed to do the job.

By the time he had repaired the engine, he had learned a great deal about it—and it seemed to him that most of what he learned was bad. He thought the engine was slow and inefficient.

"I should think," Watt said to himself, "that a good mechanic could improve that engine." And then he smiled. "I'm a pretty good mechanic myself. I think I'll try."

For years he experimented, making one model after another. None of them quite satisfied him.

"It's still too slow," he said. "Waiting for the steam to cool off each time takes much too long."

Suddenly he had an idea. Why wait for the steam to cool off, to bring the piston down? Why not *force* it down, with steam blown in from the top of the cylinder—just as it was forced *up* by steam?

He started to build still another model, cutting each piece of metal by hand, and laboriously fitting them all together. And finally one day it was finished—ready for trial.

Steam shot the piston to the top of the cylinder. Instantly another gust of steam shot it down. Back and forth the piston flew—so fast that Watt could hardly believe his eyes.

He had done it. He had invented an engine that was much more powerful, much more efficient, much faster than the best Newcomen engine ever built.

The news spread quickly. James Watt was besieged by mine owners begging him to build engines for their mines. He and a partner went into the business of making what came to be known as the Watt engine.

Steam-driven wheels replaced water wheels

Large engines or small—they could build any size that was ordered. And Watt figured out a system that helped mine owners decide how big an engine they needed: he learned by careful experiment how much work a single horse could do, and he called that amount of work *one horsepower*.

Then he asked each mine owner, "How many horses would you need to do the job?" And if the mine owner said he thought fifty horses could do it, Watt made him a 50-horsepower engine.

Whenever we measure things by horsepower today, we are using a term which James Watt gave us.

Watt gave the world one more important thing too: when he connected his piston to a wheel, men everywhere realized that this steam-driven wheel could replace wheels driven by water.

Now at last factories and mills could leave the crowded

river banks. Man finally was able to create his power wherever he needed it.

And when man mounted the steam engine on a carriage, he made the first steam locomotive.

Branca's Engine Becomes the Turbine

But as time went by people began to wonder if it wasn't possible to turn a wheel *directly* by steam—without the use of a piston that went up and down. And they remembered Branca's funny little engine for pounding drugs; the steam from the statue's mouth had blown a wheel around.

It wasn't easy to apply Branca's idea to a big, efficient engine. Men worked on the problem for nearly a hundred years.

Charles Algernon Parsons, an Englishman, finally solved it in 1884. He built an engine in which steam pushed directly against a wheel. Parsons' wheel was of a special kind; it was composed of hundreds of blades fastened to a shaft, and enclosed in a metal casing.

We call this kind of engine a *turbine,* from the Italian word *turbino,* meaning *whirlwind.* The action of the steam against the blades does make a kind of whirlwind of motion, and the wheel revolves very rapidly. But it moves so smoothly that if we put our hands on the outer casing, we can feel scarcely any vibration.

Turbines are particularly useful for driving our great steamships and the tremendous electric generators that supply our country with light and power.

Electric Power

About 2,500 years ago a Greek scientist named Thales rubbed cloth briskly against amber—and found that the amber suddenly had the power of picking up, or *attracting*, light objects.

We can repeat his experiment today, even without a piece of amber. Hard rubber or plastic will do as well: rub an ordinary fountain pen against cloth for a few moments, and the pen will pick up a scrap of paper.

Thales's discovery was neglected for over two thousand years. But about 1600 an English scientist, Dr. William Gilbert, also noticed amber's power to attract. He talked to others about it, and they agreed to call this power *the electric*, because the Greek word for amber is *elektron*.

People grew curious about the electric—or *electricity*, as we call it now. They learned that they could produce it in other ways, and that it was sometimes accompanied by tiny bright sparks. These sparks seemed to them particularly interesting. They learned that if they walked across a thick rug, for example, and then touched a door-knob, they might see a spark jump from their hand to the knob. They discovered that human hair sometimes crackled and gave off sparks when it was being combed.

All this seemed very amusing. Somebody even invented a machine—a large disk spinning between brushes—that made quantities of the long leaping sparks people loved to watch.

Demonstrations of the machine were given before

large audiences. People applauded when sparks were used to explode gunpowder, as a special feature of the show. The host at an elaborate dinner entertained his guests with a display of sparks shooting out from the dishes on the table.

But not everyone treated electricity as a joke. Some scientists studied it carefully and seriously.

Storing Electricity

In Leyden, Holland, Pieter van Musschenbroek decided to study the effect of electricity on water. He connected a water-filled jar to a spark, or electric, machine, and then spun the disks rapidly for several moments. When he touched the jar a very startling thing happened: he was knocked down!

Van Musschenbroek realized that he had stored up a great deal of electricity in his jar—enough to produce a powerful shock.

Other scientists heard about what he had done, and soon they too were storing up electricity in what they came to call Leyden jars.

Benjamin Franklin, having received several of these jars as a gift, immediately began to experiment with them. He learned that several Leyden jars, connected together, could store up far more electricity from an electric machine than one jar could.

And then Franklin found the answer to a question which had puzzled scientists for quite a while. Were flashes of lightning during a thunderstorm, and the tiny sparks from an electric machine, both caused by the same

Franklin's kite catches lightning

thing? Was lightning really just a very large "spark" of electricity?

Franklin connected one of his Leyden jars to a kite string, and sent his kite aloft during a thunderstorm. When the lightning flashed, his jar was immediately filled with electricity. Franklin had proved that lightning and electricity *were* the same.

The Frog Legs Jump

In Italy, about 1780, a man made a mistake—and it brought about important results.

The man was Dr. Luigi Galvani, a student of anatomy. He was studying the behavior of the muscles in frogs' legs. And one day he took several frog legs out of the salt-water in which he kept them, and hung them up on copper hooks. When his steel knife happened to touch one of the legs, the leg twitched—as if the muscles in it were still alive!

Galvani couldn't believe it. He touched the leg again with his knife—and again it twitched.

50

And so he sat down to think about this remarkable thing. He knew he could make dead muscles twitch by connecting them to an electric machine. He had done that many times. But his electric machine was nowhere near the frog leg hanging on its copper hook.

Then what had made it twitch? Galvani decided he had discovered a new kind of electricity—and announced to the world what he called "animal electricity."

Volta's Battery and Current Electricity

Another Italian scientist, Alessandro Volta, read what Galvani had said, and decided Galvani was mistaken.

"There is no such thing as animal electricity," he said to himself. "The frog leg was wet with salt water. It was hanging on a copper hook, and Galvani touched it with a steel knife. Perhaps copper and steel, separated by salt water, will make electricity."

He tried it, and found out that he had guessed correctly. He could make electricity by placing paper, dampened in salt water, between sheets of copper and steel.

Then he found that sheets of copper and zinc, separated by paper moistened with acid, made even more electricity. Soon he was making piles of thin copper and zinc sheets, separated from each other by acid-soaked papers. And the taller his pile, the more electricity it made.

Volta had invented the *battery!*

And he had given the world a new *kind* of electricity: it wasn't all used up in one flash, or spark, like the electricity from a spark machine or a Leyden jar. Instead it flowed steadily, like a current of water. It came to be called *current electricity*.

Volta's invention of the battery opened up a whole new world for the scientists of the year 1800. Suddenly they thought of electricity in a new way: as a force that might be used to do useful work.

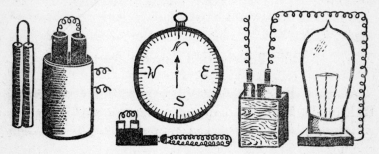

Current electricity does useful work

They performed hundreds of experiments. They learned that electricity could travel over wires—could be carried swiftly from one place to another. They learned that it could produce both light and heat.

But electricity was far too expensive to be practical. Batteries wore out quickly. And when they wore out they couldn't be repaired; they had to be thrown out, and new ones built. Even the most hopeful scientist admitted that if electricity were ever to take a place beside steam and water power, some cheaper way of producing it would have to be found.

Fortunately man was soon to learn how to make it, much more cheaply and in enormous quantities, out of coils of wire and magnets.

Electricity and Magnetism

More than two thousand years ago, in a part of ancient Greece called Magnesia, certain rocks had been found which could pick up, or attract, iron. They came to be called *magnets,* after the place where they were discovered.

A chip of this stone, floating on a cork in a bowl of water, would always point to the north—and thus magnets were used to make the first compass. Later it was discovered that a needle would also act like a magnet, if it had been first rubbed against a piece of magnet stone. By the year 1800 all compasses were made with needles which had been rubbed against magnets. We call such needles *magnetized.*

It was one of those needles that pointed the way to the cheap new method for making electricity.

Dr. Hans Oersted, a Danish scientist, was lecturing to his class one day, in front of a table holding a compass, a jumble of wires, and a Volta battery. One of the wires connected to the battery happened to slip out of Oersted's hand and fall across the compass.

Instantly the compass needle, which had been pointing north as usual, swung wildly out of position.

Oersted stared. He moved the wire away—and the needle returned to the north. He put the wire back again —and once more the needle jumped out of position.

Oersted didn't know why the needle had jumped. But he thought it might be important. He wrote a careful report, in which he said that there must be some connection between magnetism and electricity.

André Marie Ampère, in France, read that report in 1822—and immediately set to work.

Within a very short time he proved that Oersted was right; there was indeed a connection between magnetism and electricity. A coil of wire *when it had electricity flowing through it,* would act just like a magnet. It would turn toward the north just as a magnet did.

Ampère announced his startling discovery to other scientists: electricity could produce magnetism!

The Magnet Makes Electricity

Across the Channel in England, the brilliant and amazing Michael Faraday read Ampère's statement over and over. And then he asked himself a question: if electricity could produce magnetism, could magnetism produce electricity?

Faraday was the son of a blacksmith, poor and without education. But, even as a boy, he had been so determined to become a scientist that he persuaded Sir Humphry Davy, president of the Royal Institute of London, to give him a job as bottle washer in the Institute laboratory.

Davy himself was the most famous scientist of his day, and highly honored for his many important discoveries. But when someone once asked him which of his discoveries had been the most important, his answer was "Faraday." The young bottle washer lived to become as famous as Davy himself.

Faraday had no interest in wealth. He wanted only to learn—and everything he learned, he gave freely to the world. When he set out to answer the question he had asked himself, he hoped to give the world a valuable gift: a cheap method for producing electricity.

And he succeeded. For years he experimented with magnets and coils of wire. And finally, in 1831, he built a small machine, operated by a hand crank, which actually produced a current of electricity from those wires and those magnets.

The current was so feeble that Faraday could scarcely measure it. But his little machine was not a battery, which would quickly wear out. It would make electric current as long as it was cranked.

Faraday had made the first *electric generator!*

Power from Electricity

Others eagerly followed the road he had marked out for them.

It was a hard road, with all sorts of unexpected obstacles. Nearly forty years went by before Z. T. Gramme, a Belgian, built a really practical generator: it produced electricity cheaply and efficiently.

But much else had been accomplished during those same forty years. Inventors had been working on devices for *using* cheap electricity as soon as it would appear. Out of their work came the electric motor and the electric lamp.

In 1879, at an industrial exhibition in Berlin, people watched amazed as a small railroad train glided smoothly around its circular track. Its engine didn't pant and chug; it gave off no clouds of steam and smoke. The silent invisible electric power that drew the train along was carried in the tracks beneath the wheels.

In that same year the American Thomas Edison startled his neighbors in Menlo Park, New Jersey: he lit his laboratory with the first successful electric lamp. It was only a small glass globe, but the tiny loop of thread inside it, heated to a white heat, shed a brilliant glow. On New Year's Eve crowds of people came to Menlo Park on a special excursion train from New York City, to see the miracle of houses and streets lighted by electricity.

The visitors were so enthusiastic that Edison soon built a huge generator in New York—a generator big enough to supply power for thousands of lights. By 1882 a whole section of New York City was blooming with Edison's shining electric globes.

Factory owners began to ask for electricity to replace their cumbersome steam engines, their huge steam boilers that must be constantly tended and fed with fuel. So larger generators were built, in central locations. Wires carried the electric power to hundreds of factories miles away.

Within a few years electricity was doing a large share of the world's work.

The Explosion Engine

It must have seemed, for a while—from 1850, say, to 1900—as if all the inventors in the world were working on electricity. Edison alone in his lifetime took out more than 1,200 patents on his inventions, and most of them had something to do with electricity.

But certain inventors in that period were interested in other things—even in other kinds of power. They were trying to invent still a different sort of engine.

They knew exactly the kind of engine they wanted to make: it must be light in weight, it must be movable, it must not be attached by wires to a generator, or any other distant source of power. It must be able, like a steam engine, to create its own power—but without boilers and fires.

Such an engine would be especially useful, they thought, to drive the wheels of a *light* carriage. It could transform the light carriage into a horseless carriage, as the steam engine had long ago transformed a *heavy* carriage into a locomotive.

Looking back into history they found that two men had been working toward just that kind of an engine nearly two hundred years before. The men were Papin, who invented the piston, and a Dutch scientist named Christian Huyghens.

Huyghens was interested in almost everything. He improved the telescope and invented the swinging pendulum still used in clocks. When he learned about Papin's steam-driven piston, he experimented with an engine that was driven, not by steam, but by gunpowder. An explosion of gunpowder in the end of the cylinder drove the piston upward—just as gunpowder drives a bullet from a gun.

He and Papin worked together on this idea for quite a while, but finally gave it up. They hadn't been able to figure out a way of quickly "loading" their cylinder with gunpowder, over and over again, to make the piston move rapidly back and forth.

The First Gas Engine

Huyghens' explosion engine interested Étienne Lenoir very much, when that French scientist began his experiments about 1855. Lenoir, too, thought a piston could be driven by an explosion—but he thought gunpowder wasn't the right material to use. So he built an engine similar to the Watt steam engine, and tried to operate it with *gas*.

The gas—like the gas we cook on today—entered the cylinder and was exploded by an electric spark. The explosion drove the piston up. Another explosion at the top of the cylinder drove it down. One after the other, in quick succession, the explosions sent the piston back and forth.

Lenoir's engine worked. He even used it to turn the wheels of a horseless carriage. But people laughed at his clanking, clattering contraption and Lenoir grew discouraged.

Other inventors, however, felt that Lenoir had been on the right track. Several Germans were soon working along the lines he had suggested. By 1876 a German named Nicholas Otto had built an engine that was much smoother and more efficient than Lenoir's had been.

But even Otto's engine had two drawbacks: it got too hot; and the gas it used was both dangerous and troublesome.

It was Gottlieb Daimler, in 1883, who overcame these two difficulties. He invented a way to keep the engine cool by circulating water around the hot cylinder. And he invented the *carburetor*—which made it possible to replace gas with liquid fuel such as kerosene, benzene, naphtha and gasoline.

Daimler's improved engine was what all the inventors had been working toward. And it was so small and light that he installed it on a bicycle—and the world had its first motorcycle. The world's first gasoline-driven automobile was made at about the same time, by still another German named Carl Benz.

The gasoline engine proved useful in all sorts of other ways too. It did the work that small steam engines had been doing. Steam rollers became gasoline rollers. Steam shovels became gasoline shovels. Great lumbering steam-driven farm tractors became small powerful gasoline-driven machines.

The gasoline engine today supplies power for machinery in many places where electricity isn't available. It operates generators which *make* electricity—so that homes and farms far from electric lines can have lights and refrigerators.

And the gasoline engine also made the airplane possible.

The Diesel Engine

But nobody tried to use the gasoline engine for big jobs —such as pushing ships and heavy locomotives. The fuel a gasoline engine used was too expensive for that.

A German named Rudolph Diesel, thinking about that fact one day, decided to try to make an engine that could use a cheaper fuel. He thought of the cheap coal used to heat the boilers of steam engines—and put finely powdered coal dust into an engine he had built. But when he exploded it, the engine blew up and Diesel nearly lost his life.

He refused to give up, however. And by 1892 he had patented what we call the Diesel engine. It had all the

Diesels for ships . . . jets for planes

advantages of a gasoline engine, but it was as cheap to run as a steam engine because it used cheap crude oil as its fuel.

Soon Diesel engines of 5,000 and even 20,000 horse-power were being built and used to run great ships and locomotives. Large Diesels are driving generators in many huge power plants throughout the world today— and smaller Diesels have proven to be economical power for busses and trucks.

Jet Power

The very largest engines in the world today are still steam-driven and water-driven turbines—descendants of Branca's curious little engine designed in 1630.

And our most recent source of power, the jet, is a de-

scendant of an even older engine—the toy spinning ball
Hero built in 120 B.C.

Hero's steam engine was spun around by jets of steam
spurting out of the bent arms of the ball. Today's powerful jet engines are driven forward by the tremendous
force of jets of flaming gas shooting rearward. Jet-propelled planes can move even faster than sound—and
sound travels 12 miles in a single minute!

Atomic Power

In recent years, man has discovered still another source
of power—atomic power—that may be the power of the
future. How it will be employed is still uncertain.

The word *atom* comes from the Greek word *atomos*
which means *indivisible*. As long ago as 500 B.C. a Greek
philosopher named Democritus explained the nature of
the universe by saying that all substances were made up
of tiny particles—atoms—and while he made no attempt
to prove his theory in a laboratory many of his ideas have
been proved true in modern times.

Although atoms are so unbelievably small that no one
will ever be able to see one, scientists today know that
they in turn are made up of still smaller particles, and are
now able to "smash" atoms.

When an atom is shattered, the most tremendous ex-
plosive power the world has ever known is released. So
far the chief use that has been made of this power has
been in the manufacture of atomic bombs. But scientists
promise that more constructive uses for atomic energy
will be perfected in the future. It may well be that this

new form of power will one day do most of the world's work.

The heat of atomic explosions may be used to make steam—to drive enormous steam turbines.

Or inventors may devise an engine that can be driven directly by the power of the shattering atom, without using steam at all.

We can't be sure what form the future power will take. But we can be sure that it will have its roots in the work of past inventors—perhaps even in the work of inventors who lived earlier than Hero himself.

4. GOING PLACES

"Let's go!"

How many times a day those words are said!

We go—all of us—on foot, on bicycles, in cars and on trains. We go in rowboats and ocean liners. We go in airplanes.

But walking, of course, was man's first way of going places.

Probably his next way of going was by boat.

Man traveled over the ground and over the water for many hundreds of years before he learned to travel through the air.

Traveling over the Ground

We know that primitive man was often hungry, because the animals that he tried to catch for food could run faster than man himself. But he finally tamed some of those swift animals, and learned to ride on their backs. Then he could travel as swiftly as they could.

And then man invented the wheel, and learned to use it in all sorts of ways. He made two-wheeled carts and carriages, then wagons and larger carriages that rode on four wheels.

But for thousands of years, he had only two ways to turn his wheels: by man-power or by animal-power.

When slaves were plentiful, human muscle pulled even the heaviest loads. But as slaves became scarcer, animals did more of the work. They were still pulling most of the world's burdens a hundred and fifty years ago.

But animals were expensive. They had to be fed and taken care of whether they worked or not. And animals became tired. They might be able to go fast at the beginning of a journey, but their legs grew weary and they went slower and slower, and finally they had to stop.

People often said that what the world needed more than anything else was a horse that never got tired. But usually they said it as a joke. They didn't think such a thing was really possible.

The Iron Horse

And then the steam engine was invented. The first really good one, made about 1770 by James Watt, was used to pump out the underground water in coal mines so that miners could work in safety. Watt himself thought that perhaps his engine might also be used to turn the wheels of a carriage, but he didn't take the idea very seriously.

Others did. Here, they thought, was what they had been dreaming of: a power that never grew tired. They began to think about ways to put this "iron horse" to work.

A Frenchman named Nicolas Cugnot put a heavy

steam engine on a curious three-wheeled wagon—and the engine pushed the wagon along the road!

"But it's crazy, Nicolas," his friends told him, laughing. "Look! We're walking faster than your horseless carriage can go. And besides, it stops so often! It stops almost the minute it starts!"

"But not for long." Nicolas had to shout at them over the roaring of his engine. "It always starts again as soon as I make more steam."

"But it looks so funny!" they told him.

Cugnot didn't even hear them. He was trying to turn his big awkward engine around a corner.

It couldn't be done. The engine fell over into the ditch instead, with a great crash.

People said Cugnot and his engine were a public danger. Poor Cugnot was thrown into prison.

But it is Cugnot we remember today, and not the men who laughed or those who had him arrested. Because Cugnot's horseless carriage was the ancestor of today's railroad and today's automobile.

The railroad came first.

The Steam Locomotive

Richard Trevithick was born in England at about the time Watt was making his steam engine. So when Richard went to work in the mines, as a boy, the puffing steam engine was one of the first things he saw. He thought it was the most interesting thing in the world.

At night, when he went home, he made little steam engines of his own and experimented with them.

And finally, in 1804, he too made a horseless carriage—a big steam boiler set on wheels. It could go faster than Cugnot's and the steam power didn't give out so quickly. But even so it never went very far without stopping.

"It's not the engine's fault," Trevithick said. "It's the fault of the roads. Look at them—full of holes and ruts! And when it rains . . . !" He shook his head. No steam engine in the world, he thought, could ever pull a carriage through that deep sticky mud.

But Trevithick could never remain discouraged for long. A moment later his eyes were twinkling. "I'll just ask the government," he said, "to lay wooden floors over the roads. Then . . ."

Suddenly he stopped. Perhaps what he had said wasn't so funny after all.

He had remembered the wooden tracks, or rails, that were always laid in coal mines, so that the small coal carts could be pulled easily over the rough mine floor. Trevithick decided that if he could run his horseless carriage on similar rails, most of his troubles would be over.

Three years later he had made what he called a steam *locomotive*. It had to have rails to run on—but it could go five miles an hour, pulling five wagons, ten tons of iron and 70 men!

Thirteen years later, in 1817, an English coal mine foreman and an English mining engineer—Timothy Hackworth and William Hedley—made a locomotive with a tall smokestack. The coal fire under their steam boiler burned so well, with that smokestack, that the engine puffed strongly and steadily along. It was nicknamed the *Puffing Billy*.

And in 1829 George Stephenson, another Englishman,

exhibited his famous locomotive called the *Rocket.* It went 29 miles an hour!

The Steam Railroad

The men who owned the horse-drawn carriages and freight wagons and stagecoaches of the day declared that steam locomotives were dangerous. They said passengers would be scalded by the steam, that sparks from the smokestack would set fire to farmers' fields, that the steam engine might blow up. They wanted people to go on using horses.

But the public was no longer so afraid as it had been in Cugnot's day. All over England tracks were laid down. And all over England people began to ride the steam cars —first as an experiment, for the thrill of rocketing through the countryside at such a speed; and then simply as a convenience.

Coal mines began to work harder than ever, to supply enough fuel for the greedy locomotives. Business boomed. Goods could be carried quickly from mine to factory, from factory to town, from inland to seaport. England— and with her the whole continent of Europe—entered a new period of prosperity.

America Needs Railroads

But in this country the coming of the railroad was even more important.

In 1820 the United States was still a young country. It

had great riches—especially in the newly settled lands along the Ohio and Mississippi rivers. But the new nation needed trade routes. Grain and meat from the river valleys had to be shipped to the towns along the Atlantic coast. Manufactured goods from the towns had to be shipped westward. And in 1820 there were only two paths for this commerce. Both of them were very slow.

One was by water—down the Mississippi to New Orleans, and then along the coast to Baltimore or New York. That journey took several weeks.

The other was over the government's new National Road, from Cumberland, Maryland, to Wheeling on the Ohio River. The road builders had used the *macadam* method recently invented by the Scotch engineer, John McAdam: they had laid large stones on the bottom of the roadbed, with smaller stones on top of them and still smaller stones on the surface.

Horse-drawn stagecoaches rolled over the new highway every day—but eight or ten miles an hour was considered a good speed. The big Conestoga wagons—the great freight carriers of the day—needed two weeks for a trip from Baltimore to Wheeling.

A third route—the Erie Canal, connecting the Hudson River and Lake Erie—was already being prepared. But even when it was finished, in 1825, travel remained very slow; horse-drawn canal boats, even the fastest ones, could move at only five miles an hour.

So it's not surprising that certain Americans, hearing about England's new steam railroads, decided that America needed railroads too. The brilliant John Stevens built a circular track in his own yard, in Hoboken, New Jersey, and then built a locomotive to run on it—so that

his friends and neighbors could see for themselves how
practical a railroad would be.

Early railroad train

Stevens' brother-in-law, the influential Robert Livingston, argued the question with him. He told his own
friends—influential, like himself—that railroads were foolish, and he managed to block the railroad for several
years. But finally Stevens convinced hard-headed businessmen that the railroad was a good investment.

Things began to happen fast.

The Tracks Are Laid

The first tracks for the Baltimore & Ohio line were laid
in 1828, and within a few years other railroads were
started.

They were to be the lifelines of the new country, tying
it together, uniting scattered settlements into a strong
nation. Wherever rails were laid, new towns sprang up.
Trade increased. And as the railroads grew, the country
grew with it.

On May 10, 1869, when the tracks of the Central

Pacific joined the tracks of the Union Pacific line at Promontory Point, Utah, it was possible to travel by railroad all the way from the Atlantic to the Pacific Ocean.

In forty years American railroads had grown from a pigmy to a giant. And that amazing growth was possible only because of the inventiveness of the men who made railroad equipment. They designed and re-designed— they built and re-built—always improving, always keeping up with the need for safer and faster transportation.

The Rails

America's early rails were made of wood, covered by a thin layer of iron. But Colonel Robert L. Stevens, John Stevens' son, developed a T-shaped solid iron rail and soon solid iron rails were being used all over the world.

When steel-making improved, and steel became plentiful, rail-makers used this new stronger metal instead. And rails got bigger too, in order to carry the heavier locomotives and cars that were being made.

Today a single yard of mainline rail may weigh over 100 pounds.

The Engines

America's first locomotives—like her first rails—were imported from England. But this state of affairs didn't last very long.

Peter Cooper, of New York, built the tiny *Tom Thumb* for the Baltimore & Ohio line. Two watchmakers—Phineas Davis and Matthias Baldwin—turned their delicate mechanical skill to the making of locomotives. Big iron foundries also entered this booming business. Each man learned from the other's mistakes, and gradually engines grew better and better.

Each of the early engines was given a warm welcome by the public, and an affectionate nickname: *Old Ironsides, Experiment, Hercules, The Best Friend of Charleston.*

The Passenger Cars

In the beginning passenger cars were ordinary carriages or stagecoaches, equipped with new wheels to fit the tracks, and connected to a locomotive.

After a while special passenger cars were built—long boxes, with windows in the walls and rows of bare boards for seats. A coal stove at one end of a car heated it in winter. Crude early sleeping cars had three tiers of wooden bunks, without sheets and without mattresses.

George M. Pullman, trying to sleep in one of those bunks, decided that something had to be done about the discomforts of overnight travel. In 1858 he invented what we call the *Pullman.* It had more comfortable beds, was lighted with candles, and had two washrooms.

More recent Pullman cars, and ordinary passenger cars as well, are as luxurious as small hotels on wheels. They have upholstered seats, carpeted floors, curtained windows and excellent lighting.

Of course pioneer railroad travelers had no diners on their trains. They either brought their food with them— or they didn't eat. Some trains managed to stop quite regularly at restaurants where the passengers were al-

lowed to rush out and buy themselves a meal. But the
diner, as we know it today, wasn't invented until after the
Pullman car.

The Freight Cars

All the first freight cars were simply heavy wagons or
heavy platforms on wheels. One of these wagons, directly
behind the engine, carried the wood for the steam boiler's
fire. The cars were small and the wood supply didn't
always last out the trip. But trains didn't run on regular
schedules in those days, and the engineer could easily
stop long enough to go into the woods and cut down a
tree or two.

Later these wood-carrying cars became a part of the
locomotive itself—the part we call the *tender*.

As the railroads began to carry a greater variety of
goods, however, special freight cars were invented for
special kinds of cargo. The refrigerator car, invented by
Gustavus Smith, made it possible to ship things like fresh
fruit and vegetables, fresh milk and meat, for many hundreds of miles.

Today the usual freight train is made up not only of
box cars and flat cars, but also of mail cars, of hopper cars
for coal and gravel and ore, of stock cars for live cattle,
and tank cars for gasoline and other liquids.

Lights and Brakes

Trains once ran only in the daytime; they had no way
of lighting up the track ahead. The first train headlight

was simply a blazing bonfire, built on a sand-covered flat car attached to the front of the locomotive. But oil lamps soon replaced the fire. And finally electricity replaced oil.

And some of the early trains had no brakes at all. When they approached a station the engineer would blow a whistle and reduce his speed—and people at the station would rush out to grab the cars wherever they could, hanging on hard until the cars slowed to a stop.

The first real brakes were foot brakes. When the engineer pressed on a pedal with all his weight, wooden blocks rubbed against the locomotive's wheels and slowed them down. The next improvement was to put brakes on each car. Brakemen applied them by hand, at a signal given by the engineer's whistle.

But cars grew heavier. Locomotives increased in size—could pull more cars at a higher speed. Hand brakes were no longer strong enough to stop a train—especially if it had to be stopped in a hurry. Accidents occurred more and more frequently.

Young George Westinghouse of Schenectady, New York, became interested in the problem when he saw two trains collide, head on. It was a clear day, and both engineers had signalled for brakes. But neither train was able to stop in time to avoid the wreck.

Westinghouse tried to figure out a method by which an engineer could, by himself, instantly apply brakes to every car of a train. When he was still only 23 years old he opened a factory to manufacture the new air brakes he had designed.

They didn't work very well at first. Twenty years went by before Westinghouse had a brake that satisfied him—

and the American railroad. He also manufactured signals for the elaborate warning system that the railroads gradually adopted, and switches to permit a train to move from one track to another. But his perfected brake was his greatest contribution to railroad safety.

Today air brakes are used on all trains, and on many heavy busses and trucks as well.

Now a network of steel tracks connects the smallest village with the largest city, carries thousands of tons of freight and thousands of passengers daily. Not all our huge modern locomotives run by steam. Some are powered by electricity or Diesel engines. But they are all, nevertheless, descendants of Nicolas Cugnot's first gasping "iron horse."

The First Automobile

The story of the automobile also begins with Cugnot's "iron horse"—but the second chapter wasn't written for a long time. We already understand the reason for that: we know that even Trevithick's improved engine was so heavy that it bogged down on the bad roads of that time.

And, once locomotives were invented, people weren't much interested in trying to improve the roads. By 1890 there were more than 160,000 miles of railroad track in the United States alone—but when a doctor set out on his calls he still had to hitch a horse to his old-fashioned buggy.

One by one the men who tried to make steam-powered carriages gave up, defeated. And then finally, in Germany about the year 1885, Gottlieb Daimler built his gasoline motor. It was so light that it could even be used on a bicycle—transforming that bicycle into the world's first motorcycle.

Carl Benz, another German, built a similar motor and used it successfully on a very light three-wheeled carriage.

By 1892, in France, gasoline-powered carriages were being offered for sale.

Suddenly most inventors seemed to realize that the gasoline motor was the answer to their problem. Not all of them were convinced, of course. Even years later, especially in the United States, a few steam-driven cars were being made. In fact the Stanley Steamer and the White Steamer were so light and silent and fast that their American builders believed they were better than the early gasoline cars. But the public never much liked the idea of having to wait until the water in a boiler got hot, before a car could start. And it was the public which finally decided in favor of the gasoline engine.

The American Automobile

In a barn in Springfield, Massachusetts, in 1892, Charles Duryea and his brother Frank fastened a small four-horsepower motor under the seat of a light buggy— and made America's first real automobile.

They steered it with a kind of stick, or tiller, and it chugged noisily as it bumped down the street on its big buggy wheels. But their "buggynaut," as they called it, weighed only 700 pounds: they knew that if it got stuck in a hole they could, if necessary, lift it out.

People stared at them and laughed. Probably the Duryea brothers were the first to hear that famous scornful question, "Why don't you get a horse?"

In Detroit, Michigan, the very next year, a young engineer for the Edison Electric Company said to his wife over the supper table, "Clara, I'm going to try it out this evening!"

Early automobiles

His wife knew what he meant. She had watched Henry Ford at work in his little shop every evening for a month.

"Will it be safe—at night?" she asked.

Henry Ford smiled. "The streets are less crowded at night than they are in the daytime," he said. "There won't be so many people around to laugh at me."

But he didn't have to worry. His little "gasoline buggy" ran smoothly out of the small brick shop, riding high on its four thin bicycle tires, and ran smoothly up the street.

The automobile wasn't a success overnight. Most of the early ones cost so much to build that only the wealthy few could afford them.

Ransom Olds was the first manufacturer who wanted to make cheap automobiles, so that many people could buy them; but the other men in his company thought his plan was foolish. And so it happened that Henry Ford was the first to make really inexpensive cars in large quantities.

In 1908 he made and sold over 8,000 Fords—and the day of the automobile had really arrived.

The early Ford, like all other early cars, had to be cranked by hand before it would start, and that was a back-breaking job. But in 1912 C. F. Kettering invented the self-starter, and after that even women could drive automobiles.

Automobile makers did their best to make the riders comfortable. They put springs under the seats. French rubber manufacturers named Édouard and André Michelin invented a fat air-filled rubber tire that helped to cushion the bumps. But nothing the car builders did could overcome the miserable roads of the day—the same bad roads that had postponed the automobile's invention.

By 1920 there were nearly ten million car owners in the United States alone—and all of them were complaining about the roads. And so at last—*because* of the automobile—those roads were remade.

Smooth asphalt or concrete was laid over rocky macadam surfaces. Broad paved highways replaced narrow rutted lanes. Curves were straightened out, for safety, and traffic lights and road markers sprang up everywhere. The automobile was changing the face of the world.

Today there are many millions of automobiles in the United States—and millions of auto trucks and busses as well. They crowd the roads night and day, carrying freight and passengers everywhere.

Today the making of automobiles is one of the country's largest industries, and automobiles are a vital part of our everyday lives.

Nicolas Cugnot would certainly open his eyes and stare if he could see today's millions of sleek automobiles and motor busses, and today's mammoth motor trucks, all—like the streamlined railroad—the children of his first "iron horse" that ended its brief career in a ditch.

The First Boat

Long before there were any roads in the world at all, man traveled by water.

He watched a log floating down the river, and saw that it didn't sink. And the next time a log came by, man grabbed at it, hauled himself astride and rode with the current.

He had his first *boat*.

It would only float downstream, of course. But man soon learned to cut a branch, paddle it in the water, and push his log back up against the current.

Hollowed-out logs came next. Some of them were carefully burned out, some were chiseled away. Certain primitive tribes today still make slender swift canoes out of a single log.

Several logs or poles fastened together made another early kind of boat. We would call it a *raft*. And we know that rafts were probably made six thousand years ago by the Egyptians living along the Nile. But the first rafts were awkward to handle, and were mostly useful for traveling downstream.

Early man discovered that blown-up animal skins would also float, and this helped him to understand that the lighter his craft was, the easier it was to push. So he cut more wood out of the center of his log, until he had only a very thin shell left.

And finally he learned to make that shell in other ways. He fitted animals skins over a light wood framework, making a boat much like the kayak the Eskimo still uses today. American Indians used great sheets of birch bark, neatly cut and sewed together over a frame of slender bent sticks. Or man made his whole boat out of strips of wood, pegged together.

Four Important Things

Man had to invent four simple things before he had a boat that was really useful: the oar, the oarlock, the anchor and the rudder.

Man's early paddle—like our canoe paddle today—*pushed* a boat along. It was an important moment when some long-ago inventor realized that *oars,* which *pulled* a boat forward, could do a better job. Man could put the full strength of his back into the job of rowing with oars—and could therefore make his boat go much faster.

But the oar had to be held in place on the boat, so he invented the *oarlock.* Probably the first one was merely a notched branch pegged to the side of a boat.

The *rudder* was the next important step. A canoe could be easily steered by the paddler. A rowboat could be steered by pulling harder on one oar than the other. But larger boats needed a special steersman for the job. He stood in the stern of the boat and held an oar in place as a steering device.

Finally some clever boatman figured out that the

steersman's oar could be securely hinged to the boat—and then the hinged oar changed its shape and became the rudder. The gigantic rudder on the *Queen Mary* today is simply a development of that simple idea.

Probably man's first *anchor* was a heavy stone or an animal skin weighted with rocks or sand. But either of those things might be dragged along the bottom of the water, if a boat was heavy or if there was a swift current. Man realized that he needed some kind of a hook or prong, to hold his anchor—and his boat—in place.

About three thousand years ago a bent rod was used, and a few hundred years later an anchor with two prongs, or *flukes,* was invented. Legend tells us that the first one was made by the Greek wise man, Anacharsis—and that our word anchor comes from his name.

When man finally had oars, oarlocks, rudders and anchors, he was able to handle larger boats and take longer trips.

Sails to Catch the Wind

The Chinese were probably the first to use a sail—to let the power of the wind do some of the work man had been doing with his own muscles.

The Chinese sampan, a kind of light skiff with a single sail, is still in use today. But the sampan also has an oar, so that it can be rowed along.

The Phoenicians and the Egyptians learned to use sails too—but their early sailing ships likewise had oars, because in the beginning sails were only useful when a ship was going *with* the wind.

It was a long time before man learned to turn his sails, so that they could catch a wind blowing from any direction—or, as sailors say, from any quarter. This meant that oars and oarsmen were no longer needed. This was the only important improvement man made in his ships for many hundreds of years.

He experimented with the number of his sails, and with the shape of them. But in 1492, when Christopher Columbus set forth, his *Santa Maria* looked very much like an

Early sailboats needed oars too

ancient Phoenician sailing ship and it took him three months to cross the Atlantic Ocean.

The very finest of all the sailing ships was the clipper. It was long and slender, with a sharply-pointed front, or prow, so that it slipped smoothly through the water. Its three masts were very tall—sometimes 150 feet high—and they might carry as many as twenty sails. Clippers were so fast that some of them could cross the Atlantic in less than ten days.

The clippers were the last and best of the sailing ships. But even the clipper couldn't move through the water if there was no wind. By the time man had learned to make the swift clipper, however, he was also learning how to make his boats move without any sails at all—without depending on the wind.

The Coming of the Steamboat

We have seen how people laughed at the first horseless carriages. We remember that Cugnot was put in jail.

So it's not surprising that the first steamboats were also laughed at. Some governments even passed special laws against them.

Papin, who invented the piston—before the steam engine itself had been perfected—put a paddle wheel on a boat in 1707 and turned the wheel with steam power. But when he attempted to try out his invention in Germany, the law said he couldn't use his boat on any river in the country.

In England and France and the United States other men also experimented with steam-driven paddle wheels and other devices. But they too had troubles.

In some cases their steam engines were so heavy that their boats sank immediately. Even when the boats would float, they moved very slowly. People said that they were dangerous because they might blow up—and some of them did. Most of the early inventors grew discouraged and gave up.

One of the men who didn't give up was William Henry, of Lancaster, Pennsylvania. There were a lot of good mechanics in that town during colonial days. And Henry, although he never made a successful steamboat himself, talked about the subject all his life. Some of the people he talked to caught his own enthusiasm, and tried to make boats of their own.

James Rumsey, one of his friends, made a boat which traveled four miles an hour. George Washington is said to have watched it with great interest as it steamed up the Potomac River about 1786.

Another of Henry's friends was John Fitch. Fitch and a watchmaker, Henry Voigt, spent many years trying to make a good steamboat. They had to make their engines by hand, with poor tools and poor material. Finally, in 1790, they built a steamboat which went seven miles an hour! But they had to give up working on it when their money ran out.

Money was usually one of the great difficulties for the men who were struggling to invent a good steamboat. A steamboat cost a great deal more to make than most inventors were able to scrape together. So it's fortunate that three wealthy men—one Englishman and two Americans—finally became interested in the idea of steam-driven boats.

The Englishman, Lord Dundas, owned part of a busy canal through which ships were pulled by teams of horses. Lord Dundas decided that a steam-driven tug might do the work better, and he asked a Scotch inventor named William Symington to tackle the problem.

In 1801 Symington invented a tug so powerful that it could pull two large ships at once. It wasn't used very long: Lord Dundas's partners didn't agree with him as to how valuable it was. But Symington had proved that the steamboat could be useful.

The wealthy Americans who became interested in the steamboat were John Stevens, of Hoboken, and his brother-in-law Robert Livingston, of New York—the same two men who later argued so violently about the railroad. They quarreled about the steamboat too.

Stevens had some very clever ideas about how a steamboat should be built, and he found a young mechanic named Nicholas Roosevelt to help him work them out. Together they completed several boats.

But just as Stevens was ready to put his boat to work on the Hudson River, he learned that the State of New York had promised Livingston that he alone could run steamboats on New York rivers for the next twenty years!

Disappointed and angry, Stevens took his boat, the *Phoenix*, out into the Atlantic and down the coast of New Jersey to Philadelphia. And although his boats never became popular, Stevens and Nicholas Roosevelt were proud that their ship had been the first steamboat to venture out into the ocean.

Stevens would be even prouder today, if he could know that huge ocean liners use screw propellers modeled largely after the device he had designed for one of his boats—although John Ericsson, who patented a screw propeller in 1836, is sometimes called its inventor.

In the meantime Robert Livingston had decided that the public was ready for steamboats. First he persuaded New York to give him the right to operate all steamboat traffic in the state. Then, while he was in Paris as ambassador for President Thomas Jefferson, he began to look around for a designer to make the kind of boat he wanted. The man he chose was brilliant handsome young Robert Fulton.

Fulton had been born in Lancaster, where during his boyhood he had heard about steamboats from William Henry. And although Fulton had later gone to Europe to study painting, he was always interested in mechanical things. He designed a dredge for canals, a kind of torpedo and a crude submarine which he offered to Napoleon for the French government. When Livingston asked him to go to work on a steamboat, he agreed enthusiastically.

The Clermont *was a success*

He learned all he could about the boats other men had made, and then he designed the *Clermont*. The engine for it was made in England, by the famous James Watt and his partner, and the boat was built in the United States. It was 133 feet long, with a big paddle wheel on each side. The big cabin had berths for passengers.

Its first trip was up the Hudson River in August of 1807. The *Clermont* ran well and steadily, traveling the 150 miles from New York to Albany in 32 hours.

And Livingston had been right; passengers might call the boat Fulton's Folly, but they were still eager to travel on her—even though the fare of $7 was considered very expensive. The *Clermont* was a success. From the very beginning she brought fame and money to Livingston and Robert Fulton.

And then Nicholas Roosevelt launched the *New Orleans* at Pittsburgh. All the way down the Ohio River, and on down the Mississippi, people gathered along the banks to watch her go by. She reached the mouth of the river safely—and then came back up, past snags and rapids and against a heavy current.

Roosevelt's courage—like that of his great-nephew, Theodore Roosevelt, years later—gave courage to others. America's rivers became major highways of traffic.

Steamboats got larger—grew to huge two-decked floating palaces, belching smoke and sparks from two high smokestacks. Thousands of pioneers headed westward in their comfortable cabins, and thousands of tons of freight were carried on their broad decks.

Steamboat pilots were heroes, and steamboat races—like the famous one between the *Natchez* and the *Robert E. Lee*—were described in every newspaper of the land.

And when steamboats took to the ocean world commerce entered a new era. By 1860 even the flying clippers were being left behind.

Today, of course, our ocean liners weigh thousands of tons, and the largest ones can carry hundreds of passengers. Ships are made of steel, according to plans which guarantee safety, speed and efficiency.

We still launch our ships with ceremony and excitement. And when we go aboard a ship—whether it's a small chugging ferry or the largest luxury liner—we feel a sense of adventure. We can almost guess how early man must have felt, clinging to his first floating log and drifting downstream into strange and unknown lands.

Travel Through the Air

Travel by water is almost as old as man himself. Travel by air is still very new. But even early man dreamed of flying. There are legends that tell how, thousands of years ago, people attempted to soar through the air like birds.

About the time that Columbus was discovering America, another Italian—the famous artist Leonardo da Vinci —drew some careful plans for wings, and even made some models of flying machines. But even though da Vinci was almost as great a scientist as he was an artist, he never really discovered how to fly.

Today's gliders are modern copies of some of man's first attempts at flying. And some glider-makers—even among the early ones—learned a great deal about their imitation bird wings: how to turn and tilt them, to catch the wind. But none of them were ever able to fly *without* the wind. Wings alone were not enough for real flight. We know today that there must also be a motor, for power.

But before man had invented a motor that would lift his wings, he did learn to do a certain kind of flying—or floating—through the air: he learned to make balloons.

The Floating Balloon

Balloon-makers weren't trying to copy birds. They were trying to copy clouds. And their problem was to make something lighter than the air itself, so that the air would hold it up.

One day in 1783 two French brothers, Joseph and Étienne Montgolfier, noticed that smoke always floated upward.

"If we filled a large bag with smoke," one of them said, "perhaps it would float upward too."

They made a huge paper bag, built a fire under the open end of it, waited until the bag filled with smoke—and watched it rise up off the ground!

They tried it with a larger paper bag, and finally with a huge linen one. Each time the bag rose steadily upward.

They knew by then that it was hot air and not the smoke itself that was causing their bag to rise: hot air is always lighter than cold air. They knew too that their balloons would always come down because the air would eventually cool off. But they continued their trials, and the public crowded around to watch.

Finally the brothers sent up passengers, in a small basket tied to the bottom of their bag. The first ones were a rooster, a duck and a sheep—and they all landed safely after drifting half a mile through the air.

Their next passenger was a friend who was either very brave or very foolish—a young man named Pilâtre de Rozier. But de Rozier came down safely too, and had enjoyed his ride so much that he began to make balloons of his own.

In 1785 a balloon filled with gas instead of hot air, made by the Frenchman Jean Blanchard, crossed the water between France and England. People were very excited when he landed safely. But Blanchard said he hadn't been worried: he had been carrying a queer umbrella-shaped object which he said would have saved him if the balloon fell. Blanchard had invented the *parachute!*

Americans saw their first balloon when Blanchard came to this country. In 1836 Germans saw the dramatic landing of a balloon that had carried twelve passengers a distance of five hundred miles from England.

And finally, in 1852—when the steam engine was being used on locomotives—still another Frenchman, Henri Giffard, hung a steam engine beneath a long balloon which looked somewhat like our dirigibles today. Giffard wasn't sure the balloon would lift the heavy engine off the ground, but it did. And when he got up in the air he discovered that he could move in any direction he pleased. This was a great advance, because up to that time balloons had always drifted wherever the wind sent them. A person going up in a balloon had never known where he would come down!

Alberto Santos-Dumont, a Brazilian, was the first to use the lighter gasoline motor in his balloon—or airship, as it was called. And from then on all airships used this new kind of motor.

Some of the biggest dirigibles in the world were those designed by the German Count Ferdinand von Zeppelin. He was a retired army officer who had fought with the Union Army during the American Civil War, and then returned home. His dirigible was called a zeppelin.

It wasn't a single balloon, but many separate bags of gas held together by an aluminum frame covered with cloth. And it was much safer than any balloon that had ever been made, because if one of the bags was injured,

89

the rest of them could still hold the balloon up in the air.

But by the time man had learned to fasten a gasoline motor to a balloon, he had found another and better way of using that motor; he had invented the airplane.

The Airplane

A few men had tried to put wings on one of those first heavy steam engines, but their attempts were all sad failures. It was difficult enough to make a steam-driven car-

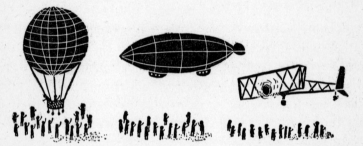

Man learned to float like a cloud . . . and fly like a bird

riage; it was impossible to make a steam-driven glider.

It was the invention of the small light gasoline engine which gave them new hope.

Samuel P. Langley was so sure that he could make a sucessful flying machine, and that it would be useful in wartime, that he persuaded the United States War Department to give him money for his experiments. But something always went wrong. Langley's ideas were good, but they just didn't work.

It was the famous Wright brothers—Orville and Wilbur—who turned Langley's failure into success. Their first flight in 1903 lasted less than a minute—but they were sure they could do better.

And they did. They improved their engine, and improved their wings. Five years later they were staying in the air for an hour at a time.

The airplane is one invention in which Americans always led the way. It was the American, Glenn Curtiss, who invented the first *hydroplane*—a machine which could be landed on the water. Today we have airplanes which will land on either earth or water; we call them *amphibians*.

The First World War brought about many improvements in airplanes, and gave the world many trained pilots who loved to fly.

They went on flying. In 1918 they began to carry the United States mail. In 1921 they began to fly at night, crossing the continent in twenty-seven hours, lighted on their way by newly-installed revolving beacons.

In 1926 a commercial airplane first carried paying passengers.

In 1927 Charles A. Lindbergh, with a few sandwiches and a map in his pocket, made the first non-stop flight from New York to Paris. He flew 3,610 miles in 33 hours.

Almost overnight, it seemed, flying became an accepted means of travel. Commercial airlines established routes connecting cities, countries and continents. From new airports airplanes took off, one after the other, on regular schedules. Businessmen came to realize that they could have breakfast in New York and supper in Los Angeles. International travelers could start their day in Paris and end it in New York.

The Second World War gave aviation another powerful thrust forward. Engines doubled and tripled their power. Radar penetrated fog and darkness to guide planes to their targets and safely back to their bases. Planes grew in size until a ten-ton load was not unusual.

Speed faster than sound was achieved by the use of the new jet engine.

Today great airline terminals are as large as the largest railroad stations, and operate with the same split-second efficiency. Skyliners carrying half a hundred passengers or more take off at five-minute intervals, pointing their sleek aluminum noses to the four corners of the earth. Perishable freight is delivered to waiting customers in a matter of hours. Even heavy machinery is carried by air when speed is vital.

And the small airplane has begun to take its place alongside America's family automobile. The farmer flies to town from his isolated farm. The sportsman flies off for a weekend of fishing. Doctors make emergency calls by plane into areas where there are no roads.

Hundreds of inventions made possible this rapid development of aviation. Inventors in every field—physics, chemistry, electronics, metallurgy, mechanics—played their part in the rise of this newest form of transportation.

Once man dreamed of flying, like a bird. Today he *can* fly—farther and faster and higher than any bird man has ever seen.

5. THE PRINTED WORD

Have you ever watched a newspaper being printed? Have you ever watched giant printing presses making books or magazines? If you have, you will probably never forget the sight of these great machines with their thousands of whirling parts.

We call these machines *printing presses* because they *press* the paper against the inky letters, or type. Once printing presses were very small. But over the years they grew larger and larger, until today some of them are as long as a city block and weigh thousands of tons.

Once printers had to put sheets of paper into presses by hand, one sheet at a time. Today paper comes in rolls and is drawn into the machine automatically at express train speeds. A hundred years ago it took long minutes to print one page. Today a thousand big magazines can be printed in that time.

How did man learn to build these wonderful machines —machines that today bring us all the knowledge of the world on the printed pages of books, newspapers and magazines?

Many men in many lands helped make today's printing possible. Each added a little bit to what had been done before him.

Before There Could Be Printing

Before printing could exist there had to be something to print: there had to be words. There also had to be something to print *on*—such as paper. And, finally, there had to be something to print *with*—type and printing presses.

The words came first.

The Beginning of Words

Many thousands of years ago, groups of people discovered that it was useful and necessary to agree among themselves that certain sounds would stand for certain things. The sounds were simple. Maybe at first they were nothing but grunts meaning *yes* or *no*. Then other sounds were used to stand for such things as *cave*, *fire*, and so on. Finally man could talk about everything he knew or did.

But spoken words are easily forgotten. When a hunter killed a big bear, for example, he told all his neighbors about his strength and bravery. But he feared that in a few days people would no longer remember what he had done. How could he keep his story fresh in their minds?

Picture Writing

Then he had an idea. He got a sharp stone and scratched a picture into the wall of his cave. The picture showed him killing the bear. He was sure now that whenever people looked at the picture they would remember what a great hunter he was.

This ancient hunter had invented a kind of writing. We call it picture writing. For thousands of years it was the only kind of writing people knew.

Picture writing

Even today the Chinese and certain other people—including the American Indian—use picture writing. In fact we all use it part of the time. The road markers on our highways show a wavy line which we all know means "curve ahead." And instead of writing the words "This Way" we sometimes show a picture of an arrow or of a hand with a pointing finger.

Writing by Sounds

But there is another kind of writing which we generally use today. It was invented several thousand years ago when some people got tired of having to draw a lot of pictures every time they wanted to write a message.

These people said, "Why should we draw a picture for every word? Let us instead invent signs for *sounds*, and put different signs together to make written words, the way we put sounds together when we speak those words."

Maybe it can be explained better like this. A picture writer who wanted to write the word for POT would have to draw a picture of a pot. But with the new system a writer didn't have to go to all that trouble. He knew that if he wrote a P and an O and a T, everybody would know what he meant. The three signs—or letters—stood for three sounds. And those three sounds spoken together stood for POT.

Besides, these same three letters put together in a different way could stand for TOP. And by adding one more letter he could have other words like SPOT or POTS or STOP or TOPS. The new system made writing much easier.

In our own writing we use 26 of these sound-signs, or letters. They make up our alphabet. With these 26 letters we can write all the thousands of words in our language.

We call this kind of writing *phonetic* writing. We took the word phonetic from the Greek word *phone*, which means *sound*.

Things to Write On

For thousands of years men scratched their pictures on stone, in soft clay and even on metal. In China they painted their word pictures on silk. The Egyptians invented a light-weight substance to write on which they called *papyrus,* because they made it out of thin strips from the papyrus plant. Our word *paper* is taken from the Egyptian name of this plant.

Papyrus was the best thing to write on people had ever had up to that time, and a great deal of it was made and used. Men who were specially trained for the job were hired by kings and rich men to write out laws and poems and stories. The richer a man was, the more sheets of papyrus he had written for him. The possession of many sheets of writing became a mark of wealth, like having much gold or many jewels.

In fact there is a legend about an ancient king of Egypt who was determined to have a bigger collection of writings than the king of neighboring Persia. This Egyptian king knew that the papyrus plant grew only in Egypt, and so he passed a law forbidding anyone to send papyrus to Persia.

But the Persian king had no intention of being beaten in the race for the biggest library. He instructed his wise men to find something else to write on—and they did. They discovered that the skin of young sheep and goats, cleaned and specially treated, made a very good writing material. Soon the Persian scribes were once more hard at work.

In those days Persia was called Pergamena and this name was given to the new writing material. It became even more popular than papyrus had been, and is sometimes used today for very important documents. We call it *parchment.*

The Greeks and Romans used great quantities of parchment. When they filled a sheet they would roll it up and store it away in their libraries. The Romans called these rolls *volumen,* meaning *rolled up.* Today books are often called *volumes,* from the same word.

The Invention of Paper

In the meantime the Chinese were busy inventing a newer and much less expensive writing material. They pressed tiny wet shreds of wood and grass between two screens, squeezed all the water out and then let the damp pulp dry. When it dried completely they had *paper*—the first paper in the world.

Not long after the year 700 the Arabians captured some Chinese prisoners of war and learned from them the secret of paper making. From Arabia the secret was carried into Europe.

Today we make paper almost exactly as the Chinese did, except, of course, that we use great machines and chemicals for making the paper white and smooth.

The Very First Printing

What is printing? To put it simply, printing is any means of making many identical copies of the same writing or the same picture.

Thousands of years ago, when one king sent a message to another king, he marked it by putting a blob of sealing wax on the letter and pressing his seal ring into the soft wax. In that way the king who received the letter could be sure who had sent it, since each king had his own special seal, and it always made the same mark.

In other words a seal ring was a means of making

countless identical copies of the design that was carved into it. Such a ring is really a tiny printing machine.

In that case, why didn't someone invent a real large printing machine as soon as papyrus or paper was invented? The answer is simple: for a long time there was no need for printing because only a few people could read.

Two thousand years ago only the kings, nobles, rich men and priests knew how to read, and they could afford to hire scribes to write for them. Even if they needed two or three, or a dozen copies of the same writing, it was easy to order the scribes to write it that many times.

The Romans and Greeks, in fact, sometimes had hundreds of copies made of a single book. They simply taught slaves to read and write and set them to work. Sometimes a hundred slaves would be assembled in a single huge room with a reader who slowly, word by word, read a book aloud. Each slave wrote as he listened, and when the reading was completed there would be one hundred copies of the book!

Since there were plenty of slaves and plenty of time, the Romans and Greeks were quite satisfied with their system.

Block Printing Came First

It was the Chinese who first realized that carving—such as they had on a seal ring—could be used in other ways than just for signing documents. They found that inscriptions on stones could be transferred to paper by dusting the stones with a sooty substance, pressing the paper against the stone, and rubbing the paper very hard.

Soon they began to carve pictures and bits of picture writing on stone and wood for the special purpose of transferring the pictures to sheets of paper. As far as we know, this was the first real printing.

In about the year 770, the Japanese empress Shotoku became eager to convert people to the Buddhist religion. She decided that the best way to do this would be to give her many subjects little charms—little strips of paper on which appeared a Buddhist text. She ordered her craftsmen to prepare them. Her order was carried out by the Chinese method of printing.

The word-pictures of the text were carved on a block of wood. The carving was then inked and pressed on paper. These little texts, some of which still survive today, are the oldest known printed matter in the world.

This kind of block printing became widely used in the Orient, and—because the Chinese and Japanese were such wonderful craftsmen—the work they did was very beautiful.

But about the year 1,000 the Chinese were beginning to realize that carving a whole page on a big block was a slow business. They began to look for some way of saving time.

And they found it.

Printing with Movable Blocks

It probably happened like this. One day a printer was beginning to carve, or engrave, a block of wood. He looked at the large smooth surface and he thought of all the hundreds of word-pictures he would have to carve before the block was completed. And then he said to himself, "See how many times I have to carve the word for *man*. On the blocks I carved yesterday, and the day before, there were dozens of *man's*. Isn't it too bad that I can't use over again the *man's* I have already made? That would save so much time."

But he couldn't take a *man* from a block he had made before and somehow put it into the block he was cutting that day.

Still, as he sat there slowly cutting the fine lines in the wood, he kept thinking of his idea. There were other word-pictures that were used over and over again. The words for *yes* and *no*, and *house*, and *woman* and *boy* and *girl* and many others.

And suddenly he had it! Instead of carving a whole page on one solid block of wood, he would carve a lot of single word-pictures, each on its own block. Then he could arrange the word blocks together to make a sentence, and arrange many sentences to make a page. And, after the page was inked and printed on sheets of paper as many times as he wanted, he could take all the word-pictures apart and use them over again to put together in other sentences for other pages.

He tried his new system and it worked.

He had invented little carvings that could be moved about—or what we call *movable type*. It was one of the greatest inventions ever made in the art of printing.

The First Type Mold

China's near neighbors, the Koreans, made the next big improvement in printing. Instead of pressing a page full of wood blocks against paper, they pressed the blocks into fine wet sand. This left marks in the sand which were exactly like the carved characters in the wood. Then they poured molten metal over the sand and let the metal run into every hollow. When the metal was cold and hard the Koreans had an exact copy of the original wood carvings.

This metal copy was inked and pressed against sheets of paper. In the meantime the original wood blocks were being used to form a new page. The Koreans had invented the *type mold,* an invention we use today in printing.

It is not surprising that for about a hundred years after this invention became widely used—from about 1400 to 1500—the Koreans were the best and most productive printers in the world. They even set up a government department of printing and published many books, so that everybody had the opportunity to learn the country's laws and its literature.

But in the Rest of the World

But, 500 years ago, Europe had no contact with Asia. People didn't travel back and forth between the two continents so the Europeans heard nothing about the new wonders of movable type and the type mold. Europe had hardly any printing or any books.

Indeed, Europe seemed hardly ready for such inventions. The once-great libraries of Greece and Rome had been destroyed during the terrible wars that began about the year 400, and few books had been written since that time. All during the next several hundred years—a period we call the Dark Ages—the only men who made books were a few monks. They wrote them by hand, decorating the pages with beautiful drawings in scarlet and gold. But these books were kept safely hidden from public sight.

Monks made books by hand

A little block printing was done during the latter part of the Dark Ages, but the process of carving out each separate page was so expensive that only a few wealthy nobles could afford block-printed books.

And in any case the nobles firmly believed that learning—like gold—should belong only to themselves and the church.

There Must Be Books

But about the year 1400, all over Europe, a new spirit arose. Men who had long been called peasants or serfs, and who had been treated little better than animals, began to believe that they too had rights. Out of this feeling a great new Middle Class of people was born—people who were neither peasant nor noble, but who demanded the right to live as respected human beings and the right to improve themselves.

These people wanted to learn.

Suddenly books were needed. And those men who knew how to print with blocks began to wonder how that slow method could be improved.

If only they could have been told what the Chinese and the Koreans had already discovered!

Europe's First Movable Type

It is possible that Lawrence Koster of Holland was the first European to work out the idea of movable type. But the records of that time are not clear about it.

We do know, however, without doubt, that Johann Gutenberg of Mainz, Germany, printed the western world's first complete book from movable type.

Gutenberg was an unsuccessful, middle-aged printer when he first hired an engraver to carve several sets of the alphabet. Gutenberg was much older before his first book was finshed. He had printed the entire Bible in Latin. It filled 1,282 pages!

For each of these pages he carefully arranged his letters into words, and words into lines. When a page-full of lines was ready, the type was locked into a frame, and the frame—type and all—was set into an old wine press. Gutenberg then inked the type and pressed paper against it by means of the big screw that had once been used to squeeze grapes.

Then he loosened the screw, carefully removed the

printed page, and repeated the slow process with a fresh sheet. When he had printed enough copies of that page, Gutenberg unlocked the frame and returned each piece of type to its own special box. Then he had to start all over again arranging the pieces of type to form the words and sentences for the next page.

Gutenberg died in 1468 at the age of 70. He had already been forgotten by many of his friends and was

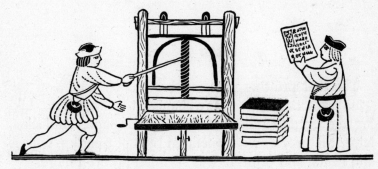

An early printing press

deeply in debt to others. The only Gutenberg Bibles which still remain in the world are worth over a hundred thousand dollars apiece today. Gutenberg's only rewards were hard work and poverty.

And Then There Were Many Books

But despite the difficulties of making books, the brave new work went forward. Within fifty years after the first printed book appeared, about twelve million books had been printed in Europe.

When the first colonists came to the new world, they brought their books with them. By 1539 a printer in Mexico had set up the western hemisphere's first press. A hundred years later Stephen Daye was establishing the first press in what would one day be the United States— in Cambridge, Massachusetts. England already had its first newspaper, Butter's *Weekly Newes*.

With each passing year there were more books everywhere. And still there were not enough.

Faster Presses

The first printing presses were clumsy copies of the wine press. Soon these were changed to permit faster inking and faster handling of the sheets of paper. And then, later still, presses were operated by foot treadles, wheels and gears, and printing was speeded up even more.

At long last, in the year 1810, steam power was applied to printing. Later on the electric motor replaced the steam engine. Huge frames of type were locked in place on these new presses, and hundreds of sheets could be printed in the time it had taken Johann Gutenberg to print one.

The Korean idea of the type mold was also put to use. Then, in 1847, printers discovered that they could place their type around large cylinders. When they made their paper in long rolls, instead of in single sheets, they could unroll it over the cylinders of type, and print at high speed.

Men learned how to make reproductions of pictures. They also learned how to have colored pages, by running a sheet through the press more than once and using a different colored ink each time.

But in one respect printing was not advancing. Men still had to build words by picking type out of a box, one letter at a time. And later the type had to be put back into the boxes the same way—one letter at a time.

Printers' Devils

Benjamin Franklin was a printer's devil—or apprentice printer—when he was twelve. He learned to set and distribute type in the same way Gutenberg had done it. His Pennsylvania *Gazette*, founded in 1728, was a small newspaper because setting and distributing the type took so long.

More than 100 years later another printer's devil named Samuel Clemens—better known as Mark Twain, the author of *Huckleberry Finn*—did these same chores for the newspaper in Hannibal, Missouri. A grown-up Mark Twain tried in vain to invent a machine to do the long slow job he had done as a boy.

As late as 1889 the largest newspapers in the world were still small compared to the ones we know today—because the setting of type was still so slow.

Printers' Delight

It was not until 1889 that the ingenuity of two men succeeded in freeing printers from the slowest of all their tasks.

One was James O. Clephane, a stenographer in the law courts of Washington, D.C. The other was German-born Ottmar Mergenthaler, who was working in Washington in his cousin's machine shop.

Clephane worked out the original idea for the automatic typesetter. Mergenthaler, with his skilled fingers and his knowledge of mechanics, transformed that idea into a real machine.

The machine is a complicated one, but it is operated as simply as a typewriter. The operator sits before a keyboard, and sets type by tapping out the letters on the keys. As each lettered key is tapped, a mold for that letter

Newspapers, magazines and books by the million

drops into a slot. When a full line has been completed, molten metal is squirted against the molds. In a second the entire line of type is reproduced—much as the Koreans made type by pouring hot metal into their sand molds. One more touch of a key and all the molds are returned to their places, ready to be used to form another line.

The name of this machine describes the way it works. It makes one line of type at a time; it is called a *linotype* machine.

And Today the Printed Word Is Strong

Today, in the workrooms of our great daily newspapers, dozens of typesetting machines click softly as their operators tap out the news of the world. The huge presses await their daily feeding of type and ink and paper.

In the workrooms of book printers and magazine printers, other men sit at other typesetting machines . . . other great presses roar and rumble . . . and then the pages are collected together, and securely bound between covers by still other ingenious machines. These are the books and magazines that fill our homes, our libraries, and our schools.

Today in our country we all learn to read as a matter of course. Automatically we turn to our newspapers to discover what happened a few hours ago on the other side of the world. Just as automatically we turn to our books to learn facts, gain understanding, increase our skill, and find fun.

And for all this we owe a great debt to many men from many lands: the first hunter who scratched a picture on his cave wall . . . the inventors of papyrus, of parchment, of paper . . . the Chinese who invented movable type . . . the Koreans who invented the type mold . . . Koster and Gutenberg . . . Clephane and Mergenthaler . . . and the thousands of others who made their contribution to the great art of printing.

These men must all have known, as we know today, that the printed word is one of man's most valuable tools for progress, one of his strongest weapons in the fight for freedom—one of his most precious possessions.

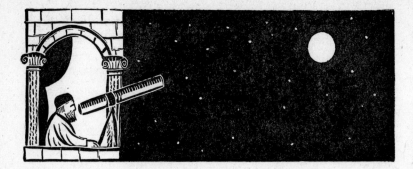

6. SEEING THINGS

Once man believed that the earth was a round ball hanging in the center of a great round dome of sky. He thought the sun and moon and stars traveled around the earth like fireflies circling an orange. Now we know that isn't so. Now we can learn the truth about the earth and its path through the sky, about the sun and the stars. We can do this because now we have the telescope.

Once man believed that sickness was caused by an angry God or an evil spirit. Today we know that diseases are caused by tiny germs, much too small for the eye to see. Today we know about these germs, and can often prevent sickness or cure it—because now we have the microscope.

Once the only pictures man could make were the ones he painted or drew. Some of them were very beautiful, but they were expensive and they never could show things exactly as they are. Today we have many pictures—we call them photographs—that show things exactly as they are. We have moving pictures too, all because we have the camera.

And although once nothing could be done for the

people who had poor eyesight, today thousands of weak eyes are helped to see better—because today we have eyeglasses.

None of these important things could be invented until we first had a *lens*.

Nature Made the First Lens

Every eye has a lens. It is the lenses in our eyes that make it possible for us to see.

If there is something wrong with the lenses of our eyes, things look blurred to us, or foggy.

Sometimes people can see only things that are very near their eyes; things farther away look blurred. When this happens we say they are *near*-sighted. Other people can see clearly only the things that are far away, while the things nearby look blurred. We say those people are *far*-sighted.

But most of us can see something one foot away—and something one hundred feet away—equally well, because the lenses in our eyes are good.

The lens in our eye looks like a small round transparent cushion, curved on both sides. If you could look at it sideways it would look like this: (). We call it a lens because its shape is like the shape of a *len*til seed.

All other lenses—the ones in our eyeglasses, our telescopes, our microscopes and our cameras—look very much like the lenses in our eyes. They too are usually round and curved, though they may be curved in different ways. But they are all transparent—we can see through them just as we see through our eyes. They are usually made of glass.

111

How We Came To Have Glass

Man has known about glass for so long that he has no record of when he first discovered it. But there is a legend about the beginnings of glass which tells how it might have happened.

The heroes of the legend are the sailors of a ship which once set out from Tyre, an ancient city on the coast of the Mediterranean Sea. The sailors were Phoenicians, and all the Phoenicians were great travelers.

On this particular trip a storm came up and the ship was wrecked. The sailors swam ashore and landed on a beach of fine white sand. They quickly built a fire with dried seaweed and some of the wreckage of their boat, so that they could get warm and dry.

Suddenly, as they sat huddled around the blaze, they noticed something strange. A little stream of shiny liquid was running out of their fire.

When the liquid cooled it became hard. They could break off pieces of it and look through it. It was glass!

Scientists today are not sure the legend is true, because glass can only be made in a very hot fire—and they don't believe that little blaze on the beach could have been hot enough. But the scientists agree that the fine white sand, and the ashes of the wreckage and the seaweed, might have contained the different things necessary to make glass.

Even today a certain kind of fine sand, called silica, is the chief ingredient of our glass.

But whether the legend is true or not, we do know that the Phoenicians were among the first people to make and use glass. They colored it for imitation jewels, just as we do today. And they learned how to melt glass and blow it into many lovely shapes. Phoenician glass became so famous that other countries were jealous.

When the Roman emperor Augustus conquered Phoenicia, in 30 B.C., he brought some of the glass-makers to

Early glass blowers

Rome and forced them to work there. Soon the ladies in Rome had beautiful glass bottles on their dressing tables, and when Romans went to a funeral they carried glass bottles to collect their tears in. Some of these tiny tear bottles—they were only half an inch tall—still exist today in our museums.

The First Eyeglasses

The Chinese, on the far side of the world, were the first to make eyeglasses, or spectacles, in about 140 B.C. The Europeans didn't make spectacles until much later—probably about the year 1300—although they had already learned how to make beautiful glass windows for their churches. They even began to make a few glass windows for houses, but these were very rare and expensive. A man who owned a glass window always took it with him if he moved to a new house, and left it in his will to his favorite son or his best friend.

In 1550 the first glass factory was started in England, and not long afterward spectacles of green glass were sold there.

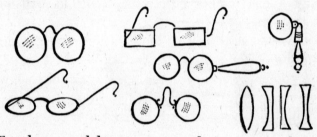

Eyeglasses and lenses were made in various shapes

Probably they weren't very good glasses, but they were supposed to be useful to people who did a lot of reading. It might seem to us that a spectacle-maker of that time would starve for lack of customers, because only a few people could afford to learn to read in those days. But the truth is that spectacles became very popular. A man wore them whether he could read or not. He hoped that if people saw him wearing glasses they would think he *could* read—and would therefore think he was wealthy!

But slowly the spectacle-makers learned how to improve those little circles of glass they were selling. They discovered that glass really helped people to see better— if the glass was curved instead of flat.

They began to make their eyeglasses, or lenses, in various shapes. Some were curved on both sides, like the lens of the eye itself. Some were curved inward, like a pillow that has been sat on; they looked like this ▭◁ from the side. Others were curved on only one side, and looked like this ▭◁ or this ◁▭.

The early lens-makers had a good time with these various shapes of glass. They discovered that when they looked through a lens that curved outward, everything looked bigger than it really was. And that if they looked through a lens that curved inward, things looked smaller than they were.

Today we call these two kinds of lenses a *magnifying* lens and a *reducing* lens, but in those early days people didn't bother with names. They just thought that while they were learning to make better eyeglasses, they had accidentally discovered some entertaining new toys.

A Man Named Galileo

The man who first showed the world how important these toys could be was an Italian named Galileo.

From the time Galileo was a small boy he loved mathematics better than anything else in the world, and all during his lifetime he was interested in figures and experiments. Galileo opened the eyes of the world to all sorts of remarkable things which nobody had ever noticed before.

One day, for example, he climbed to the top of the Leaning Tower of Pisa, with a one-pound ball of lead in one hand and a ten-pound ball of lead in the other. He wanted to prove to his teachers that they were wrong when they told him that heavy things fell faster than light things. And he did. He dropped both his balls at once—and they both landed in the same instant.

One day Galileo heard that a lens-maker of Holland—a man named Hans Lipperhey—could make distant things appear to be very close to his eye. Lipperhey did it by looking through a specially-shaped lens—one of the outward-curving ones that we call a magnifying lens. Galileo immediately ordered some of the curved pieces of glass for himself.

Galileo's Telescope

He experimented with them for a long time. Finally, one day in the year 1609, he invited a group of friends to come with him to the top of a high hill in Venice.

"Do you see any ships on the sea today?" Galileo asked when they reached the crest.

One of the friends looked out over the water. "Not a one," he said.

Galileo handed him a long tube which he had brought with him. "Look through this—and then tell me if you see any ships."

The friend held the metal tube up to his eye. A moment later he almost dropped it in his excitement.

"When I look through this tube I *do* see ships—but I know there are none!" He stared at the tube in his hand. "Is this a magic tube? Are there tiny ships hidden inside it?"

Galileo shook his head, smiling. "There is nothing inside the tube except lenses—pieces of curved glass. The ships are out at sea—miles away."

"Then how could I see them?" the friend demanded. "No one can see things which are miles away. You're trying to trick me!" And he turned angrily away.

Others looked through the tube, and also became angry at Galileo. They tried to make him admit that his tube was some kind of a trick.

But suddenly, while they were still arguing, one of them said, "Look!" He pointed toward the horizon.

Galileo and his telescope

And there—still so far away that they were only specks against the sky—were the same ships they had all seen through the tube two hours before.

"They were there all the time," Galileo explained. "But with my new spyglass we could see them long before they were visible to the naked eye. My spyglass magnified them—made them seem close because it made them seem so much larger.

"When it gets dark," he told his friends, "I will let you look at the stars through my spyglass. Then you will really be amazed. They look so close—so large. I think I will be able to learn a lot about the stars by studying them through this tube."

A Telescope Looks at the Stars

From that day on Galileo studied the heavens through his spyglass—the invention we now call a *telescope*, from the Greek words meaning *far* and *see*. He saw hundreds of stars that no man had ever seen before.

Finally he announced that his telescope had proved to him several startling things. The sun did not circle the earth, he said—as man had always believed it did. Instead the earth circled the sun. Therefore, Galileo said, the earth was not the center of the universe.

It was dangerous in those days to make such a statement. The Church had taught people that the earth *was* the center of the universe, and no one was permitted to contradict the Church. Galileo was imprisoned.

Galileo's ideas, however, remained free. They have influenced men's thinking ever since. And his first simple spyglass was the beginning of present-day astronomy—the study of the nature and the pathways of the stars.

Today we build special buildings called observatories, in order to set up our huge modern copies of that spyglass. One of our telescopes is so big that it contains a glass lens weighing twenty tons and measuring two hundred inches across.

Seeing the Invisible

Galileo had looked through his lenses at the biggest things he could see—the sun and the moon and the stars. It was some seventy-five years later before another man thought to use lenses to study things so small that the ɹaked eye couldn't see them at all—things that had always been invisible until that moment. The man's name was Anthony van Leeuwenhoek.

Van Leeuwenhoek lived in Holland, where many of the best lenses of the time were made. He was in business there, and no one knows exactly why he began to spend his evenings looking through the new toy-like bits of glass that made things seem larger than they were. We only know that he did, and that he became so interested in the game that he even began to make his own lenses.

He worked away at them very carefully, grinding smoother and smoother curves on his bits of glass, until he had better lenses than anyone else. The better the lens, the larger it would make small things seem. Finally he could make a single hair look as thick as a finger.

He looked at everything through his lenses—at the wings of bees, the legs of flies, a scrap of meat, a sliver of his own fingernail. They all looked strange and wonderful when they were magnified.

One day he decided to see what a drop of clear water looked like through his newest lens. And a few moments later he was leaping to his feet with excitement.

The Wonderful Little Animals

"There are creatures in the water!" he cried. "They wriggle! They swim about—like polliwogs in a pool!"

And then, because he liked to be scientific even though he had never studied science, he gave them a Latin name. He called them *animalculae,* which means *little animals*.

Night after night he studied the tiny new worlds which he found in every drop of water—in every drop of soup or milk or wine that he looked at through his lens. And at last he wrote a long letter about his little animals and sent it to the most important scientific society in the world, the Royal Society of England.

Most of the people who read the letter laughed. They said it was impossible that there could be animals so small that hundreds of them—as van Leeuwenhoek had said— could swim about in a drop of water. They thought the little man in Holland was simply making it all up.

Even those who believed him—who went to see for themselves the funny little creatures—thought only that van Leeuwenhoek had discovered a very curious thing. People argued about where the little animals came from —how they had got into the water and the soup—but for a long time it didn't occur to anyone that the tiny creatures might be useful, or dangerous.

In fact, as time went by, the little animals were almost forgotten. Scientists became much more interested in other things—in the newly-discovered electricity, the amazing steamboat, the roaring black locomotive. But one day nearly two hundred years after those *animalculae* were first seen, another man looked at them—and realized that they were among the most important things in the world.

Pasteur and His Microbes

This man was Louis Pasteur, a French chemist. He too was willing to work night after night to learn more about these little creatures. He decided that they turned milk sour, turned grape juice into wine and even caused disease! And he argued stubbornly with other scientists, trying to convince them that he was right.

People might not have believed his arguments. But they had to believe in the proofs he showed them.

Pasteur proved to wine-makers how they could prevent their wine from spoiling. He proved to dairymen that if they heated their milk—and killed the little animals—the milk wouldn't turn sour. He proved to doctors that certain

Small things look large through a microscope

diseases were caused by certain little creatures, or *microbes*, as he called them; and that it was possible to cure a disease if the microbes were destroyed.

Pasteur's work inspired a great many other scientists. They studied many diseases, to learn exactly what kind of microbe caused each one. And their work has made the world a much more healthy place to live in.

No longer do we have to fear such dreadful diseases as scarlet fever, diphtheria, plague, smallpox, typhoid and yellow fever. Now we know how to protect ourselves against these and many others—because we know about the tiny microbes that cause them.

The curious little Dutch van Leeuwenhoek called his

wonderful lens a *microscope*—from the Greek words meaning *small* and *see*. The word *microbe,* of course, also comes from the Greek word for *small*.

Today we can make much better microscopes than he could. Now we have lenses so powerful that we can see the tiny cells that make up the human body, the tiny molecules that make up everything we know.

Galileo's telescope, seeing far things, shows us the place of the world in the universe. Van Leeuwenhoek's microscope, seeing small things, shows us how man and his world are made, and how many wonders there are in everything.

The Very First Camera

Camera is really a Latin word, and it means *room* or *chamber*. The very earliest kind of camera was called a *camera obscura,* or *dark room*. The name gives us a hint about how the camera came to be invented.

Sometime you may find yourself in a dark room, with a single strong ray of sunlight coming in through a tiny hole. Where that ray of sunlight strikes the wall, you might then see a small "picture" of the world outside.

Hundreds of years ago several men noticed this curious fact. Some of them even built special small dark rooms, in order to experiment with the "pictures" that seemed to come in on a ray of strong light. Finally they learned that they could get much better, clearer pictures if they made the hole a little larger and put a curved piece of glass—a lens—in front of it. They brought their friends to see the little pictures they made in their camera obscura.

These men were like the lens-makers who thought the

magnifying glass was just an interesting toy. The camera obscura made very clear little pictures against a white wall. But the pictures disappeared the moment the sunlight no longer came through the hole. And what could be done with a picture that lasted for a few moments—that couldn't be picked up and put in a frame or pasted in an album?

Catching the Picture

"If we could somehow catch the picture—make it stay there even after the light is gone," people said, "it would be a fine thing." But no one knew how to do that.

They tried following with a pencil the various shapes outlined on the wall, the way we sometimes draw around a shadow. But the drawings they made never captured the special "real" look of the picture itself.

We have seen before how inventions occur only when the work of several men is put together. That's what happened to the camera. It was finally invented only after chemists added their knowledge to what was already known about the camera obscura.

The chemists discovered that certain substances—certain chemicals—turned dark when they were left in the sun.

And one day in 1794 two young Englishmen—Tom Wedgwood was 23 years old and Humphry Davy was only 16—decided that those chemicals were the answer.

"We'll smear some of this solution of silver salts on a sheet of paper," Tom Wedgwood said, "and tack the paper on the wall where the light strikes it and makes the picture."

"It might work," Humphry Davy agreed. "The paper should turn darkest where the most light strikes it, and stay almost white where the shadows are."

They tried it and it worked! When the light was gone the picture was still there on the paper—only in black and white, it is true, but still a perfect copy in every detail.

Thomas Wedgwood, son of Josiah Wedgwood, the famous pottery maker, inherited his father's wonderful factory. And Humphry Davy grew up to be one of the greatest scientists in all the world. But probably the proudest day either of them ever knew was the day they first captured on paper the picture that men had been trying to catch for hundreds of years.

Unfortunately their picture faded away after a while. It grew fainter and fainter, and finally it was gone altogether.

The Picture Is Caught

But other experimenters came along, and other chemists, and in 1826 someone invented a picture which wouldn't fade. He was a Frenchman named Joseph Niepce.

Joseph and his brother Claude had worked out all sorts of things together, including a velocipede which was the father of all our bicycles. And finally Joseph discovered the right combination of chemicals to make a lasting picture.

He talked about what he was doing to the shopkeeper from whom he bought his materials, and the man said, "That's odd! Another fellow buys chemicals from me for the same sort of experiments. His name is Louis Daguerre."

The shopkeeper tried to bring the two men together, and finally succeeded. Daguerre and Niepce became partners. The lasting picture they finally worked out together became known as a daguerreotype, and was extremely popular. They made it not on paper, but on a thin copper plate.

Daguerre—who had been a struggling scene-painter before his remarkable success—set up a studio and fashionable people flocked to him to have their daguerreotypes made. They had to sit perfectly still for nearly half an hour, their heads clamped in a metal holder to prevent them from moving. But they thought it was worth while because Daguerre's pictures were so life-like.

Early photography was a serious business

"Look!" they'd exclaim. "Even the eyelashes are clear —and the pattern of the lace in my collar!"

Daguerre used a black box fitted with a lens, instead of the original dark room, and his system was copied in almost every city of the world. Many people today treasure daguerreotypes of a great-grandmother or a great-grandfather, looking rather stiff but very proud.

Cameras for Everybody

Naturally Daguerre's success and the popularity of his pictures encouraged many other people. New methods of picture-making were developed, cheaper and faster than the old ones. Cameras were invented that could easily be carried from place to place, that could be used outdoors or indoors.

During the Civil War a pioneering photographer named Mathew B. Brady traveled from one battlefield to another, taking pictures of soldiers in action. He was the forerunner of our news photographers today. Brady carried all his equipment in a specially-built wagon, where he printed his pictures after he had taken them.

The small handy camera that so many of us own today was finally developed by an American, George Eastman. When his Kodak was put on the market it was suddenly possible for everybody to be a photographer.

Two things—the little roll of film in the camera, and a special kind of paper on which pictures could be printed cheaply and easily—changed picture-making into a simple task. We don't have to sit still for half an hour to have our picture taken today. It can be taken in a snap—which is why we sometimes call our pictures *snapshots*.

And recent developments have made it possible for us to take colored pictures as easily as black-and-white ones.

The Picture That Moves

Today we also have motion-pictures—though probably few of us know that Thomas Edison, inventor of the electric light, was among the early scientists who made these possible.

A motion-picture camera is like an ordinary camera, except that it takes pictures very quickly, one right after the other. To make a movie of a fly walking down this page, for example, it would take one picture of the fly as he crossed the first line at the top of the page, and then another as he crossed the line below, and another for each

The picture that moves

line. Then that strip of pictures would be run through what we call a *projection machine*. This machine shows the pictures on a screen—very quickly, one after the other, just as they were taken. And on the screen the pictures seem to run together, to make one *moving picture:* the fly appears to be walking down the page.

So it is easy to see that our newest inventions can be traced back to some of the very earliest ones. The lens and the glass out of which it is made are still helping us to see our world—and to capture today's world in pictures, so that we can see it tomorrow and far into the future.

7. HEARING THINGS

"Call me soon," your friend says, as you separate to go in opposite directions—perhaps to homes that are miles apart. "I'll talk to you tomorrow," you answer.

If an early Greek or an early Roman could have heard your conversation, it would have meant only one thing to him: that you and your friend were going to see each other the next day. It would never occur to him that people could talk to each other unless they were in the same room—unless they were close enough to see each other and hear each other's voices.

Today, of course, we have the telephone. We talk to each other across thousands of miles of space—across whole countries and wide oceans.

And today we have the radio too. We sit in our living rooms, in any one of the 48 states, and hear jokes being made in Hollywood or New York.

Today we even have television, which means that we can see as well as hear those distant comedians.

And also, today, we have an invention which makes it possible to receive a message over a long distance: we have the telegraph.

All of these things would have seemed like crazy dreams to that early Greek or Roman. In fact they still seemed like crazy dreams to most people less than two hundred years ago.

The First Postal Service

Of course it was many thousands of years ago—before the days of the Greeks and the Romans—that man first wanted to send a message to someone in another town or another country. He solved his problem very simply—if not very well. He hired a swift runner, repeated the message to him until the runner knew it by heart, and sent him off. Sometimes the messenger had to travel for a hundred miles on foot to reach the end of his journey. There he repeated the words he had learned—and returned with the answer.

Things became a little simpler when man knew how to write. Then he could put his message on paper, and give the paper to a runner. Then he could be certain that nothing would be forgotten—that the whole message would be received safely.

About 2,500 years ago the Persians had a great many of these runners, stationed along all the important routes of the Persian empire. The man at one station, or post, carried a message swiftly to the next station; and the runner there set off with it to the third post. Finally the Persian runners themselves came to be called *posts*, from the posts at which they were stationed. We still use that word today when we speak of *posting* a letter, or of the *postal* service and the *post* office.

The Pony Express in the days of our Western pioneers was the same kind of postal service.

Early Methods of Signaling

In some countries, where there were a great many hills, men didn't have to run with their messages. They simply stood on hilltops and shouted their words across. And thus, from hill to hill, a message reached its destination.

The Pony Express . . . and Indian smoke signals

Finally men discovered how to send messages from one hill to another even when they were so far apart that their voices couldn't be heard. They used signals that could be *seen*.

We all know how the American Indians used puffs of smoke from their campfires for signaling. A large puff meant one thing, a small puff another, a group of three puffs something else. The early Greeks signaled by a similar method, using flaming torches instead of puffs of smoke.

Finally in England, in 1684, a Dr. Robert Hooke built a new kind of signaling system. He made large wooden letters, each as tall as a man. Then he rigged up a pulley, so that he could haul his letters high off the ground. By lifting them up, one at a time, he spelled out words.

Hooke set up several stations for his pulleys, and messages were sent from one to the next. The public was delighted with what it called Hooke's *telegraph*—a word made up out of the Greek words for *far* and *write*.

But about a hundred years later a Frenchman, Claude Chappe, improved Hooke's system. He used a pole, with a hinged crosspiece that could be pulled by strings into various positions. Each position stood for a letter of the alphabet.

Chappe's poles were very tall, and his messages could be read for some distance. By using many poles, he could send messages from Paris to Lille, 130 miles away. And by putting lights on his poles he could send messages even at night.

Today when Boy Scouts and Girl Scouts spell out words by holding flags in various positions, they are using the same sort of method that made Chappe's poles successful.

We call it the *semaphore* method, from the Greek words for *signal* and *bearer*.

One of the chief duties of the Signal Corps of the United States Army used to be the sending of messages by this system. Crossed signal flags are the insignia of the Signal Corps to this day.

The Electric Telegraph

We would probably still be using Chappe's telegraph if men had not learned a great deal about electricity. One of the things they learned was that electricity could be made to travel along a wire.

In Albany, New York, a young man named Joseph Henry made a remarkable toy with wire and electricity. Henry had worked his way through the Albany Academy and later became a teacher there, but he was more interested in his experiments than in his pupils.

One day, in the year 1831, he took a piece of wire a mile long and ran it around and around one of the rooms of the school. Then he started a current of electricity through his wire from one end—and found that he could make a bell ring at the other end.

A year later, on the deck of a small ship slowly crossing the Atlantic to New York, a group of men were discussing recent experiments with electricity—the work of the Frenchman André Ampère and the Englishman Michael Faraday. Some of the men aboard the *Sully* were scientists, but one of them was an artist—a successful painter and the president of the National Academy of Design. His name was Samuel F. B. Morse.

"It seems to me," Morse said, "that it ought to be possible to send messages over wires, by using electricity."

"Nonsense," one of the others said. "People have already tried it—and failed. If you were a scientist you'd know it couldn't be done."

"Just you wait," Morse said. "I'll show you. I'll do it."

The other passengers smiled and shook their heads. They told Morse he was a good painter—and that he ought to stick to what he knew.

When Morse landed in New York he settled down to his job as professor of design at New York University. But he talked to people who knew a great deal about electricity. He bought chemicals for batteries, and miles and miles of wire. And he began to spend all his spare time experimenting with them.

For a long time he had little luck. And then one day somebody told him about Joseph Henry's ringing bell, and Morse said, "That's just what I needed to know. Now I can do it."

Dots and dashes spell out words

He made new equipment. He used little clicking noises instead of a ringing bell. And he worked out a code with those little clicks.

One short click and one long one (Morse called it one dot and one dash) stood for the letter A. One short click, or dot, was E. Two dots stood for I.

"I've done it!" Morse said. "I can write the whole alphabet this way—and that means I can write messages."

But to prove to the world that his electric telegraph would work over long distances, Morse needed a great deal of equipment—which meant he needed a great deal of money. He tried everywhere to get that money—in the United States, and then in most of the countries of Europe, and then in the United States again.

Finally, at the end of eleven years, he persuaded the United States Congress to vote him $30,000. With this money he laid an electric wire all the way from Washington, D.C., to Baltimore, Maryland—a distance of forty miles. And in 1844 he sent over that wire the world's first electric telegraph message. The words that the little dots and dashes spelled out are still famous: "What hath God wrought."

Laying the Atlantic cable

Before very long a network of wires went up in many countries. New York could send messages to San Francisco. Paris could send messages to Rome.

"If we could only lay wires across the ocean too," people said, "the whole world would be tied together."

"Why can't we?" asked Cyrus W. Field. "We'll load a ship with two thousand miles of heavy wire and sail across the ocean, reeling the wire out as we go."

People assured him it wouldn't work—that the wire, or cable, would break before he got halfway across. And they were right.

More than once Field had to turn back, discouraged, leaving an expensive length of cable lying useless on the bottom of the sea. But each time he managed somehow to obtain more money and started out again, with a new length of cable on his ship and hope in his heart.

At last, in 1866, he succeeded. A single unbroken cable stretched clear across the ocean. And New York could send messages to Paris or London or Rome. The world was indeed tied together as it had never been before.

The Telephone

In the meantime, in a chilly attic in Salem, Massachusetts, another man was experimenting with electricity. He was Scotch-born Alexander Graham Bell.

Bell's father was a speech expert, who became famous for being able to teach the deaf to speak. As a young man Bell worked with his father.

He knew that children usually learn to speak by repeating the words they hear; but that because a deaf child never hears words, he must be taught by some other method. A deaf child has to learn to make certain sounds by learning to move his lips and tongue and throat muscles in certain ways. Bell would teach a child to say *ah,* for example, by placing the child's hand on his throat and letting him feel the way the throat muscles quiver, or vibrate, when that sound is made.

Bell knew all about the vibrations, or waves of sound, that make up our speech. He knew that if you hold a tin pot lid in front of your mouth when you speak, the lid will quiver, or vibrate, as the waves of sound strike against it. And he knew that when those vibrations strike against an eardrum, they produce sound—just as sound is produced when a bass drum is struck.

And one day it occurred to Bell that these vibrations might be carried along an electric wire. He was so excited he could hardly sleep that night. Because he knew that if he could send vibrations along a wire, he could send speech.

Other people, all over the world, had been working along the same lines. But it was Bell who finally succeeded. In 1876 he patented the first *telephone*—a name made out of the Greek words for *far* and *sound*. Here indeed was an invention that could carry sound a long distance—and it seems curious to us now that for years few people were interested in this remarkable device.

It's true that it wasn't perfect in the beginning. Voices came out of it sounding queer and cracked.

Eventually however the telephone was improved, until today there are many millions of telephones, in homes and offices in every country, all over the world.

Alexander Graham Bell became very wealthy, and he used a great deal of his money to help those who could not hear or speak. His wife had been one of his students when he was a young teacher of the deaf. He had taught her to speak—had given her a voice. And when he invented the telephone he gave the world a voice too—a voice that can be heard anywhere, across mountains and seas and continents, clear around the globe.

Messages Without Wires

Meanwhile some scientists suggested—among them Joseph Henry in Albany, and Morse and Thomas Edison—that wires were not necessary for the carrying of electricity. They thought that electricity could travel through the air by itself.

A scientist named Heinrich Hertz finally proved that electricity spread out through the air in little waves, like water spreading in a saucer. He named those waves Hertzian waves.

But Hertz was interested only in discovering and proving things—not in putting his discoveries to practical use.

The man who made a practical invention out of those Hertzian waves was young Guglielmo Marconi.

Marconi was the son of a wealthy Italian father and an English mother. The family lived on a beautiful estate near Bologna, and Marconi had the best of everything, including the best tutors. But the only thing he ever really wanted to do was to study science. As a boy he read about Benjamin Franklin's famous experiments with lightning and a kite—and insisted upon climbing up to the roof to try the same experiment for himself.

And when Marconi first read about Hertzian waves, in a magazine, he could hardly wait to get to the laboratory he had rigged up, in order to try some new experiments.

The first thing he did was to repeat what Hertz had done. And things happened just as Hertz had said they did. When Marconi made a small electric spark in his apparatus on one side of the room, his apparatus on the other side of the room "caught" it—and the same kind of spark appeared there! The electricity had traveled across the room—without wires.

"If it will travel across the room, it will travel across miles of space," twenty-year-old Marconi thought, and he begged his father for enough money to buy materials for bigger experiments.

Two years later he was proving how right he had been; he was in England giving demonstrations to important scientists. By changing his sparks into little clicks, he was sending messages in Morse code—sending those messages for miles.

In 1898, when Marconi was still only twenty-four years old, he was famous all over the world; he had sent a message, without using wires, from France to England.

Three years later he succeeded in sending his first message across the Atlantic Ocean.

An early radio set

Marconi's *wireless,* as he called it, made it possible for a ship at sea to talk to wireless stations on land—and to send for help immediately if the ship was in trouble. His invention made ocean traveling much safer than it had ever been before.

The Radio

The clicks of the Morse telegraph had become the voice of the telephone. In much the same way the clicks of the Morse code over the wireless became the voice of radio.

An English engineer, John A. Fleming, who had worked with Marconi, invented the *radio tube,* which caught the electric waves. An American named Lee De Forest invented the amplifier, which strengthened the faint electric signals into sounds that could be clearly heard. Other scientists added their knowledge, the results of their experiments.

By 1920 radio stations were set up—and people were eagerly buying the first radio sets.

Sound—and pictures too—through the air

Suddenly, as if by magic, an ordinary living room could become a theater, a concert stage, a lecture hall. Music and speeches and plays from all over the world could be heard by patients in hospitals, by housewives at work, by children in school. People on the loneliest farm could turn a knob—and invite famous singers and actors into their homes.

Radio tubes and amplifiers also made the once-silent motion picture able to talk and sing.

Television

Television, developed a few years later, made it possible to see as well as to hear over many miles of space. It too came about only after the work of many men had been put together—after countless experiments had been made and millions of dollars spent.

Scientists who had studied light, those who had studied sound and those who had studied electricity were all important in the making of successful television. By 1926 television was already a fact, but about twenty years passed before it became widely used.

People like to say that books are friends—you can turn to them whether you are happy or sad, and they are always ready for you. But we have other friends too—friendly voices that are always ready to speak to us.

The voice of a neighbor may speak to us over the telephone, from half a block away; the President of the United States may speak to us from his study in the White House; a singer may be heard from halfway round the world.

We can hear them all, because electricity brings them all to us—and because many men worked together over the years to invent the telegraph, the telephone, the wireless, radio and television.

8. MAKING THINGS

In the early days when families grew all their own food, all their clothes were made at home, too.

Animal hides were tanned to make leather, and cut and sewed to make the heavy sandals or shoes each member of the family wore.

Each family raised its own sheep, sheared their wool, spun thread out of the wool and wove it into cloth. And then the women cut and sewed the cloth into garments.

Tending the sheep and shearing their wool was not too difficult a task. But spinning the thread and weaving the cloth was a job that took all the women's spare hours. They worked at it during the winter months, when there was no planting or harvesting to be done. And during the growing season they returned from the fields at night and worked by the light of burning rushes.

It took many yards of woolen thread to make a single garment. The man who had more than one shirt or one pair of trousers, the woman who owned more than one dress, was considered very fortunate—and very rich.

People have been weaving cloth for thousands of years —perhaps since they first watched a spider weaving its

141

web. In China, long ago, they learned to unwind the fine thread out of which the silkworm spun its cocoon, and weave that thread into a delicate cloth we call silk.

In early Egypt they gathered the fluffy white cotton when it burst out of its seed pods, and drew it out into thin threads from which they could weave a fine sturdy cloth.

In South America the soft coat of the llama was twisted into thread and woven into a thick warm material. In certain other countries the tough fibers of the flax plant were made into cloth. And all over Europe cloth was made from the wool of sheep.

Sheep wool is thick and fairly long—but it is often tangled with burrs and matted with grease. It had to be cleaned and washed and combed before it could be used.

Early Spinning

When a woman had finally prepared an armful of clean wool, she tucked part of it under one elbow, drew out a pinch—as we might pull out a thin tuft from a handful of absorbent cotton—and fastened it to a hook at one end of a stick, or *spindle*. Then she set the spindle twirling, with a twist of her fingers, and let go of it. As it fell spinning toward the floor, the wool was pulled with it into a thin thread, twisted by the spin. Then she lifted the spindle and wound the twisted thread around it.

By this slow process she could make a few feet of thread at a time.

The spinning wheel was first used in India and Persia many hundreds of years before the New World was discovered. It was finally brought into Europe about the year 1300—and then brought from Europe to this country.

It was a great improvement over the simple hand-twirled spindle. The spindle on a spinning wheel was

Early spinning was slow work

revolved by the wheel's turning, and the wheel was operated by a foot pedal. The spinning wheel made thread much faster than the early spindle, but spinning was still very slow work.

Early Weaving

Looms for weaving had also been used for hundreds of years before the first American settlers brought them along to their new homes. The looms were simple frames as wide as the material to be woven. Bent nails or hooks were driven into the lower edge of the frame in a straight row. A ball of wool thread was attached to each hook. The thread from each ball was then stretched tightly over the frame, from the bottom to the top. These threads were called the *warp*.

"Setting up" a loom, as the arranging of the warp is

called, was slow and tedious—and it was just the beginning of the process of weaving.

When the warped loom was ready, it looked like a barred window, except that the bars were very close together. A new thread was used to weave in and out of the warp threads, over one and under the next, much as stockings are darned to this day. This weaving thread was called the *woof*.

Each time the woof was drawn through the warp—over and under, over and under—it had to be smoothed tightly into place before it was drawn through again.

The first great improvement on the loom was made when someone invented a system for separating the threads of the warp into two groups, and fastening each group to a bar.

To understand this important invention let's think of a warp of 100 threads, numbered for our convenience. The odd threads—the ones numbered 1, 3, 5, 7, and so forth—would all be fastened to one bar. The even threads —those numbered 2, 4, 6, 8, and so forth—would be fastened to the second bar.

When the first bar was lifted, all the threads attached to it would be pulled away from the others, making a kind of tunnel or *shed* of threads. Then the woof thread, encased in a smooth shell called a *shuttle*, could be thrown straight through that tunnel from one side of the loom to the other—and a whole row could be woven with a single movement.

When the first bar was lowered and the second bar was lifted, the two groups of threads changed places and made another tunnel. Then the woof thread was thrown back again and another row was done.

The bars were operated by foot pedals, leaving the hands free to throw and catch the shuttle.

Step on the pedal . . . throw the shuttle . . . push the woof threads tightly into place . . . step on the pedal again . . . throw the shuttle back . . . that was the slow method by which cloth was woven until about two hundred years ago.

The Beginning of the Change

By the year 1700 few men made their own shoes. In each village some man who liked to work with leather

The beginning of the change

had long been doing the work for his neighbors. They often paid him in grain or meat or cloth—the things that they had at hand.

The making of tools, the grinding of grain into flour—those jobs too had once been done in every home. But by 1700 they were also being done by blacksmiths and millers who had become expert at their jobs.

And by 1700 thousands of people, especially in England, were spending all their time spinning and weaving. They made the cloth not only for their neighbors, but for the people in many other countries; England sent cloth to her colonies on this side of the ocean, and to other lands too, in return for the goods she received from them.

Farmers and their wives were still spinning and weaving their own cloth. But in the towns and cities spinners and weavers were specialists, like blacksmiths and millers. They were poorly paid for their work. In order to earn enough to keep themselves alive the women sat at their spinning wheels and the men at their looms far into the night. And as soon as a child was old enough to operate a pedal or turn a wheel, he too was put to work to add a few more pennies to the family's income.

The time was coming when all this would be changed. And the change, when it happened, would affect a great many things in the world. It would bring about what we call the Industrial Revolution—the beginning of the world of machines we know today.

Machines caused the Industrial Revolution. The machine that really began it was a weaving machine.

John Kay's Fly Shuttle

John Kay was one of the poor busy English weavers who sat at his loom for long hours every day. His back and his arms ached constantly from the tiring process of throwing the shuttle, working the pedals, tugging down the heavy beater that tightened the last woof thread against the cloth already woven. The most tiring motion of all was the throwing of the shuttle.

He began to wish that there were some easier way of doing it—and in 1732 he had an idea.

Kay built a little box at each side of his loom, where the shuttle rested between its trips across the warp threads. The shuttle fitted neatly inside the box—like a car inside its garage—and there was also room in the box for a rod, one end of which was fastened to a cord.

When he pulled the cord, the rod jumped forward and kicked the shuttle across to the other side of the loom and into the box there. When the cord on the other side was yanked, the shuttle was kicked back again. By connecting both his cords to a single knob, Kay could throw his shuttle back and forth by simply pulling that knob.

He had built what came to be called the *fly shuttle*—and it did, in fact, seem to fly back and forth across the loom. He had also built the first of what were to be thousands of machines, each doing by mechanical means the work that human hands had done before.

Kay himself was delighted with his invention. With it he could weave much more cloth than he had ever been able to weave before.

But when the other weavers in his town heard about it, they were angry and frightened. They were afraid that the fly shuttle would make so much cloth that fewer weavers would be needed, and that many of them might starve to death. They broke into his house one night and smashed his loom.

They would probably have injured Kay too, but a few friends saved his life by carrying him secretly away wrapped in a blanket.

Kay could never return to his house or his village. In fact he was forced to flee out of England. He finally settled in France, where he died—still a poor weaver—in 1764.

But behind him, in England, his invention was not forgotten. Secretly, at first, other weavers added Kay's fly shuttle to their own looms, and earned more money because they could weave so much faster. By the time John Kay died in lonely exile, most English looms were equipped with the boxes and rods and knob he had designed.

And then many looms became idle, and many weavers were out of work. The trouble was not—as Kay's early enemies had feared—that too much cloth had been woven, but that there wasn't enough yarn to keep the weavers busy. England's spinners couldn't keep up with the faster looms. A weaver who had a fly shuttle could use up, in a few hours, all the yarn his wife could spin in a whole day and half the night.

Hargreaves' Jenny

One of these weavers was James Hargreaves. He watched his wife's nimble fingers draw out the wool as the spindle twisted it into yarn. She worked rapidly—but she couldn't work rapidly enough.

"We should have another spinning wheel," he said to himself. "Then I'd have twice as much yarn."

And then, in a single instant, the thought struck him: he didn't need two spinning wheels—all he needed was two *spindles!* And it should somehow be possible to turn two spindles with a single wheel.

Hargreaves set to work to see if he could transform his